They're Not Dumb, They're Different

Stalking the Second Tier

by SHEILA TOBIAS

An occasional paper on neglected problems
in science education

Published by Research Corporation
a foundation for the advancement of science

RESEARCH CORPORATION

A Foundation for the Advancement of Science

6840 East Broadway Boulevard
Tucson, Arizona 85710-2815

Table of Contents

Introduction

"For every complex question,
there is a simple answer—
and it's wrong."

—H. L. Mencken

To solve the nation's twin problems of a projected shortfall of science workers and general science illiteracy, many educators are proposing a massive restructuring of the curriculum and pedagogy of elementary and secondary school science. Does it all sound familiar, reminiscent of the reaction to Sputnik some 30 years ago?

While the importance of improved school science cannot be diminished and is, indeed, demanded to improve science literacy, it is not a remedy, nor does it offer hope for an immediate increase in science graduates. The author of this first of a series of occasional papers on neglected problems in science education chides members of the science professoriat for a comfortable "elsewhere" focus; for advocating K-12 reforms rather than coming to grips with the hemorrhaging of the student pipeline that occurs during the college years.

Proposed here is that science educators focus on such issues as course design, teaching and curriculum as well as on recruitment, rewards and opportunities in science. The goal would be to attract that group of able students who can do science, but select other options, a group dubbed the "second tier." By getting to get to know these students and finding ways to reverse their migration from science to other disciplines, it should be possible to stem the massive loss of potential science workers that occurs during the college years.

Such a migration reversal must take place at the several junctions at which the sciences lose potential practitioners: the transition between high school and college; the freshman year; and the midmajor, mid-decision points where, having completed as many as two years of college science, students change directions. If we are to truly alleviate the problems of an inadequately educated populace and a projected shortage of scientists and engineers, we must demand that no college student be allowed to leave science "without a struggle."

The author's previous research (see page 93 for a selective bibliography) focused on math anxiety and what makes college science "hard?" A technique she employed was the participation of nonscience faculty in artificially constructed college science lessons. In this first project for Research Corporation, she turns to introductory science as experienced by stand-ins for the so-called "second tier." Six graduate students and one professor, all from nonscience fields, were recruited to "seriously audit" introductory physics or chemistry. Their task: to purposefully explore their personal encounters with the courses and "classroom culture" of beginning college science. *They're Not Dumb, They're Different— Stalking the Second Tier* includes excerpts from the field notes of these seven auditors and comparable data from a study of Harvard-Radcliffe students who switched out of science courses, and from a University of Michigan study of a cohort of students in science.

"Final Speculations" asks penetrating questions about why the science community focuses on the supply of future science workers, while leaving demand to chance and the market. While most thinking people agree that the nation needs more science, we should not assume this need will translate into more paid work for scientists. Students (other than those singularly determined to be scientists) look for career opportunities, mobility, adequate compensation, and opportunities for advancement. If the nation is going to attract new recruits to science, we owe them not just a welcome, but jobs and career ladders appropriate to their abilities.

This essay will not be pleasing to all members of the science teaching community, and a few will complain of methodology that draws more from ethnology than the physical sciences. Such objections notwithstanding, most will agree that Sheila Tobias's findings are provocative and worthy of serious discussion. It is Research Corporation's aim to help probe the reasons behind the shortfall and the public lack of interest in science. If this booklet provokes discussion of how we can better teach and share the excitement of science, the public and our professions will be well served.

John P. Schaefer, Ph.D.
President
Research Corporation

Tucson, Arizona
May 1, 1990

Stemming the Science Shortfall at College

"Who will do science? That depends on who is included in the talent pool. The old rules do not work in the new reality. It's time for a different game plan that brings new players in off the bench."

—Shirley M. Malcom[1]

Everybody says it in one way or another: we need to teach more students more science. To a policy-oriented social scientist, this means we have to identify the able students who are choosing not to pursue science; find out why they are put off by science and attracted to other occupations; and, if necessary, change the recruitment, reward, and opportunity structures to match their temperaments and needs. This may involve providing not just more access, but more individual attention and support; not just more tutoring, but more meaningful and appealing introductory courses; not just more scholarships, but substantial loan forgiveness for those who decide to stay in science, and more and better job-ladders for terminal B.A.s; in short, substantive guarantees of *welcome* and *success.*

But "recruitment," "rewards," and "opportunity structures" are not the usual stuff of educational reform. So it should not be too surprising that science educators are promoting, rather, a massive restructuring of the nation's elementary and secondary science curriculum and the training or retraining of virtually everyone who teaches science from kindergarten through twelfth grade.[2]

I will argue here that, however necessary this restructuring may be, localism and the extreme diversity of the nation's 16,000 school districts will make precollege curricular change difficult to implement and much longer than anticipated to achieve. While such reform will chip away at science illiteracy and pave the way eventually for new

---

[1] Shirley M. Malcom, is head of the Directorate for Education and Human Resources Programs of the American Association of the Advancement of Science. This final paragraph is taken from her *Essay*, "Who will do science in the next century?" *Scientific American*, Feb. 1990, p. 112

[2] Among these are: Project 2061 of the AAAS, a new curriculum for the elementary grades that will be appropriate when Halley's comet comes around again; the National Science Teachers' Association's *Scope, Sequence, and Coordination of Secondary School Science*; NSF's $14 million support for seven projects to develop new curricular materials for elementary school science. For a comprehensive review of the more than 300 major policy studies on mathematics and science education in the U.S. since 1983, write to Jay Shiro Tashiro, Math/ Science Institute, Simon's Rock College, Great Barrington, MA 02130.

recruits to science, it may not be the most efficient or effective way to meet the projected shortfall.[3] There is no question that any shortage of science workers, actual or projected, is profoundly linked to science illiteracy. Science is too little "spoken" in the nation's households and there are too few role models for young people to emulate. Nor is there any doubt that the long-term recruitment of students to science will be served by *any* improvement in the nation's educational performance. But practically, and in the interest of cost-effectiveness, it may be better to *disentangle* the several strategies currently underway, i.e., science literacy, curriculum reform, and recruitment of future professionals to science, at least in the immediate future.

This means focusing on college.

The fact is, a very large number of American high school graduates survive their less-than-perfect precollege education with their taste and even some talent for science intact. As many as half a million students are probably taking introductory college science at some level each year. The problem is that between 1966 and 1988 the proportion of college freshmen planning to *major* in science and mathematics fell by half.[4] Even after the introductory course, the flow out of science continues seemingly unchecked. One-third to one-half of those who initially indicate an interest in science leave science well into the major, some even after completing a science degree. To stem that "hemorrhaging" of would-be science workers at the *college* level is a strategy that must be urgently pursued, along with sweeping changes in the elementary and high schools.

Why, then, has such a strategy not attracted the science community? Why the tacit approval and even preference among practicing scientists for precollege reform?[5] Some reasons suggest themselves to someone viewing the profession from outside. Reformers—and insofar as they become educational reformers scientists are no exception—are most comfortable dealing with problems that have their origins (and, hence, their solutions) elsewhere. In the case of the science shortfall, "elsewhere" is in the pedagogy and curriculum of the lower grades (where scientists have virtually no voice or influence); in the "anti-intellectualism" of the nation's home environments; in teacher-recruit-

---

[3] "Shortfall," not "shortage" is the preferred term for the anticipated difference between supply and demand for science practitioners in the next several decades. The term is generally credited to Erich Bloch, director of the National Science Foundation. Estimates of the shortfall vary from 250,000 to 700,000 B.S. (B.A.) recipients in science and engineering by 2005 amd 7,500 Ph.D's annually by that year. See Atkinson (note 14) and *The Ph.D. Shortage: The Federal Role*, report by the Association of American Universities, Jan. 11, 1990.

[4] Kenneth C. Green, "A Profile of Undergraduates in the Sciences," *American Scientist*, Vol. 77, Sept.-Oct., 1989, p. 476. Green does not point this out, but in proportion this drop occurred in all the liberal arts disciplines.

[5] There have been efforts to study and deal with the exit of science students at college, but K-12 issues decidedly dominate the national debate. See the recent *Newsweek* cover story ("How to Teach Science to our Kids," April 9, 1990). For a sampling of college-level efforts,

ment and teacher-training (which usually occur in departments of education cut off from departments of science); even in the "negative image" of scientists as portrayed by popular culture.

There may be another reason that college science teachers look elsewhere for reform. Because they are good researchers, scientists prefer situations in which variables can be isolated and controlled. As anthropologist Sharon Traweek concludes after studying the belief systems of high-energy physicists, "Scientists long passionately for a world without loose ends."[6] For many scientists, then, it seems more logical to begin with *pure substances* (the nation's six-year-olds) and *uniform initial conditions*, than to flounder in the messy bog of motivation, attributes, and prior training exhibited by postsecondary students in their early years at college.

This may be why tackling the projected shortfall through elementary and secondary school science reform is "easier" for many academic scientists to contemplate (and to ask the nation to pay for). Dealing with the problems that aggravate the shortfall during the college years is more difficult. College retention strategies cannot, however, be left to chance. Even if—especially if—the nation achieves the massive educational restructuring proposed, tomorrow's recruit to science may *not* be of like mind and motivation as yesterday's. Nor is there any guarantee that the projected shortfall will be eliminated. Restructuring or no restructuring, we need new thinking about "who will do science" and "why," thinking that may challenge college science teachers to grapple with issues they have not focused on before. These are how to recruit, teach, reward, and cultivate different kinds of students to science, students who are *not* younger versions of themselves.

But scientists are not likely to do such rethinking so long as they continue to expect the next generation of science workers to rise, as they did, like cream to the top. This is why introductory college courses remain unapologetically competitive, selective and intimidating, designed to winnow out all but the "top tier," and why, as Eric Schocket observes in his commentary on introductory physics (see *infra*), there is little attempt to create a sense of "community" among average students of science. Even good students (Kenneth Green's "B" students)[7]

see: The National Science Board, 1986 Report (the Neal Report); the NSF Disciplinary Workshops 1988 Reports; The Revised Curricular Guidelines from the American Chemical Society's Committee on Professional Training. Particularly relevant to the project detailed here is the focus on college courses in a Report of the National Advisory Group of Sigma Xi, entitled *An Exploration of the Nature and Quality of Undergraduate Education in Science, Mathematics and Engineering*, Jan. 1989. The authors of the report designate introductory courses in science, mathematics, and engineering as "watershed courses" and urge colleges and universities to make these more accessible, more interesting and more rewarding.

[6] Sharon Traweek, *Beamtimes and Lifetimes, The World of High Energy Physics,* Cambridge: Harvard University Press, 1988, conclusion.

[7] Green, *Ibid.*

are often given the wrong message that there is no room in science for people like themselves. The proverbial "look to the left, look to the right, two of your classmates will not be here after..." may have first surfaced at the Harvard Law School, but it certainly operates in introductory science where the first painful shakeout is expected to occur.

What further complicates the effort to rethink recruitment is that the "top tier" in science is characterized as much by shared values—what could even be called "style"—as by performance. Theirs is a collection of highly prized (and happily advertised) behavioral attributes that scientists like in one another and are always looking for in the next generation. As one example, the authors of a recent widely circulated study of 4,000 Ph.D. scientists and engineers, supported by NASA between 1962 and 1969, reported that "over 80 percent [of these working scientists] decided on a career in science or engineering before completing high school." Another (perhaps the same) 80 percent felt that "the intrinsic interest of the subject matter" was very important to them, and that *all other influences* (italics mine), including their high school and college teachers, were less so.

Fewer than a third of the scientists and engineers named their teachers as "significant" in their decision to do science, and even fewer claim to have paid any attention to the "prestige of science," or to its "potential for pay and promotion." Nothing, in fact, that went on in school seems to have mattered much. On the contrary, a large number of respondents remembered learning science quite as much from their hobbies as from their school work. It is clear to this reader that, for better or for worse, their relationship with science was, from the beginning, intense, private, and self-contained.[8]

From these data, the authors conclude—as do many of the experts studying the shortfall—that if the pool of science talent is to be increased, (1) more students must be attracted to science very early, "during high school or before;" and, (2) since science is essentially "practice," elementary schools should emphasize "hands-on" activities and college programs undergraduate research. Not surprisingly, these are the very activities that the scientists who designed the survey, and their colleagues who responded to it, like best.[9]

Policy analysts would not necessarily come to the same conclusions. First, "more of the same" bespeaks professional *solipsism*, i.e., ideas constrained by practitioners' own personal experiences. Second, the

[8] From the executive summary of the study, "On the Origins of Scientists and Engineers," directed by John M. Logsdon of the George Washington University Space Policy Institute, Washington, D. C. 20037.

[9] One exception to the focus on "early" recruitment is the OTA Report (*Educating Scientists and Engineers: From Grade School to Grad School,* Office of Technology Assessment, U.S. Congress, Washington, D. C., June 1988) which calls for "ongoing recruitment and retention throughout the educational process." For a concise summary of the OTA's recommendations, see Daryl Chubin, Lisa Heinz, and Robert Garfinkle, "Engineering Change in the Engineering Pipeline," *Engineering Education,* Aug. 1989.

findings are contradictory when it comes to school reform. It appears from this survey and other similar studies that scientists don't learn much science in school. So why should school reform produce more scientists? Third, the message is discouraging to all but a favored few, and the model unyielding. What we are left with after reading these biographical sketches is the strong sense that scientists are born, not made. Unless they are unusually self-motivated, extraordinarily self-confident, virtually teacher- and curriculum-proof, indifferent to material outcomes, single-minded and single-track, in short, *unless they are younger versions of the science community itself*, many otherwise intelligent, curious, and ambitious young people have every reason to conclude there is no place for *them* in science.

Science, like all professions, needs to reproduce itself nonbiologically. But by seeking attributes and attitudes much like their own, scientists inhibit recruitment from outside familiar channels. From this perspective, the low representation of women as well as racial and ethnic minorities in science may not be the result of social discrimination per se (scientists are surely too professional to discount good people because of ethnic origin, skin color, or gender, *viz.* their welcoming of "non-WASPs" to science in the 1940s and of Asians in the 1970s), but of too narrow a vision of what kinds of attributes, behaviors and lifestyles the "true" scientist displays. What we have here is an outsider-insider problem which results in a preference for "in-group" types. If strategies for solving the science shortfall are to involve the recruitment and integration of women and minorities into science, then much more than school reform and talent-searching among the out-groups for in-group types will have to take place. The science community is going to have to rework the "fit" between science and any new class of recruits—in both directions.

But what will motivate scientists to change the way they recruit and teach their subjects? At the heart of the "science education problem" in the U.S. lies a paradox. American science is, on most measures, the best and most productive in the world. For the undergraduate major in science (the student who exhibits all the right "attributes"), the training is more than adequate; for the graduate student it is said to be *sans pareil*. Foreign students flock to our graduate programs and embark on major research here because of the opportunities for self-direction, the availability of equipment, and the quality of their colleagues. Many decide to stay. David Goodstein, now vice provost at California Institute of Technology, recalls writing a memo in 1970 to Harold Brown, then president of Caltech, concerned that there wouldn't be enough American physics graduate students in future years to satisfy the needs of research universities. As it turned out, foreign students filled the gap instead.[10]

---

[10] Personal communication from David Goodstein to the author, Feb. 12, 1990.

John Rigden, director of physics programs for the American Institute of Physics, is not so sanguine about these developments. He reminds us that in 1929 I. I. Rabi, Robert Oppenheimer, and other Americans were all in Leipzig studying with Werner Heisenberg, one of the leading physicists in Germany and the world. Yet, there was only one German student in Leipzig! What the German physicists were doing for American students in the mid-1920s, Rigden says, they were unable to do for their own native sons and daughters. Rigden believes that this is the reason that by the *early* 1930s, i.e., long before Hitler depopulated German science with his racial policies, American science was in the ascendancy.[11]

While Goodstein and Rigden worry about the underproduction of American graduate students in science, other educators are concerned about the social and political consequences of foreign-dominated science and engineering education at the university level. Betty Vetter, a human resources specialist in science, reports that in some universities, English is a "second language" in science and engineering and that the reluctance of many foreign countries to send as many of their able women as men to study abroad contributes negatively to the gender balance in American research institutions.[12] Also there are no guarantees that foreign-born Ph.D.s will stay in this country.[13] Still, as many practicing scientists perceive it, the "crisis" in science education is not yet *their* problem, but rather the nation's. And they're right in the short run: it will be the economy which will bear the brunt of the science shortfall, and government and the general public the ever-increasing burden of scientific illiteracy.

So, while no reform of science education at any level can be accomplished without scientists, those of us who are outsiders also have a role to play. Any way you count them, the next real net increase in the pool of Americans willing to study and to make their careers in science will have to be "outsiders," too. If we are not to rely on the foreign-born, we need to enlarge what has hitherto been considered the natural pool of recruits to science and be willing to offer new kinds of students a welcome and a chance for success. From this will follow quite naturally more blacks, more Hispanics, more native Americans, more women, and even more (white) men, but not necessarily "more of the same."

To deal with the projected shortfall, we are obliged to think and

---

[11] Personal communication from John Rigden to the author.

[12] Betty Vetter, executive director of the Commission on Professionals in Science and Technology, mentioned as an aside during a presentation at the AAAS National Meeting, New Orleans, Feb. 17, 1990.

[13] The National Research Council's data shows that of the doctoral degrees in physical sciences awarded in 1988-89, 65.1 percent were awarded to U.S. citizens, 4.5 percent to non-U.S. citizens holding permanent visas, and 24.0 percent to non-U.S. citizens holding temporary visas; as reprinted in *The Chronicle of Higher Education*, Sept. 6, 1989, p. 16.

think hard not just about who does science and why, but who doesn't do science, and why not. To this end, we should examine, as a beginning construct, the student on the "second tier."

Defining the "Second Tier"

Are there enough qualified students to increase the ranks of science workers without compromising quality? This is the critical question, and it was posed again most recently by Richard C. Atkinson, president of the American Association of the Advancement of Science in his presidential address in February 1990.[14] The answer is we don't know very much about the *quality* of students who don't study science, but we know a great deal about their numbers.

For some years now the National Science Foundation has been publishing a "pipeline" chart based on the known numbers of individuals who, at various stages, declared interest in or earned a degree in science or engineering. The chart begins with a universe of four million high school sophomores (in 1977), of whom 750,000 claimed to be "interested" in studying science and engineering. But of these, a mere 9,700 or 0.24 percent of the original sophomore population were expected to achieve the Ph.D. degree in one of the sciences or engineering.[15]

According to the study, of the original 750,000 potential science and engineering professionals, only 590,000 would still have been "interested" during their senior high school year. And of these only 340,000 would be still committed after a first taste of college science as freshmen, a drop-off of 40 percent. Further attrition would have taken place during college. Of 340,000 declared, only 206,000 would have actually graduated in science and engineering at the end of the senior year, another 40 percent loss. And of these baccalaureates, only 61,000 would have gone on to graduate school in science and engineering, producing 9,700 completed Ph.D.s.

There are several ways we can interpret these data: one is that the falling off of interest in science is inevitable, so the most effective strategy is to increase the diameter of the pipeline and not worry so much about the leaks. Another is that those who *can* do science *will* do science. Therefore, we must beef up precollege science so that a larger proportion of entering college students will be prepared. A third way to think about the data is this: not every student who doesn't do science can't do science; many simply choose not to. What we need is a model

---

[14] Richard C. Atkinson, "Supply and Demand for Scientists and Engineers: A National Crisis in the Making," Presidential Address, AAAS National Meeting, New Orleans, Feb., 18, 1990, p. 18.

[15] Source: National Science Foundation, *The Science and Engineering Pipeline*, PRA Report 67-2 April 1987, p. 3.

that allows for more and more finely differentiated groupings among the 200,000 we lose yearly at college, groupings we might call *tiers*. From these finer groupings, could come *differentiated* recruitment, reward, and retention (and even teaching) strategies, designed to meet the needs of particular tiers of nonscience students, the tiers most likely to respond to a certain intervention and to succeed.

Many researchers acknowledge that "major losses occur during the college years."[16] Unfortunately, the pipeline model gives us only the net effects of the "dwindling supply of talent," not the reasons for the loss. Until very recently, experts simply didn't know why students leave science in college, only that they do. It was comfortable to assume that they were unable or unwilling to do the work. But one recent study appears to challenge that view.[17]

> Of the [college] freshmen who switched out of science and engineering [in 1973, 1981 and 1983], only 31 percent did so because they found the course work too difficult; 43 percent found other fields more interesting; and 26 percent believed they would have better job prospects elsewhere.

What's needed is further analysis of who doesn't do science and why not.

Stalking the Second Tier

The second tier is a loose hypothetical construct, which includes a *variety* of types of students not pursuing science in college for a *variety* of reasons. They may have different learning styles, different expectations, different degrees of discipline, different "kinds of minds" from students who traditionally like and do well at science. But then again they may not. It is important in thinking about the second tier *not* to populate it with people or even types we already know. We simply cannot predict who would be attracted by differently configured science instruction any more than we can imagine how recruitment, reward-structures and instruction in science should be changed. Hence, the initial strategy has been simply to locate a group of students who have not taken science in college and to find out what happens when they do.

We began the study by recruiting a small and diverse sample of postgraduates to stand in for the second tier. With one exception (a classicist who began science at Caltech and then quit) all had been science avoiders in college and all had demonstrated ability in other fields. Each of them was then asked to "seriously audit" a semester-

---

[16] OTA Report, *Educating Scientists and Engineers: From Grade School to Grad School*, Office of Technology Assessment, U.S. Congress, June 1988, p. 11.

[17] "The State of Academic Science and Engineering," National Science Foundation, Division of Policy Research and Analysis, in press, 1990, as quoted in Atkinson, *op. cit.*

long introductory course in calculus-based physics or introductory chemistry. They were expected to perform as well as they could in their courses, and they did. In addition, they were asked to focus their attention on what might make introductory science "hard" or even "alienating" for students like themselves.

In return for a stipend and in cooperation with the instructor, they attended all classes, submitted homework, took examinations (up to but not necessarily including the final). Throughout each course they closely monitored the instructor's style of presentation, the material in the textbook, the assignments. Most of all, they were asked to observe closely (and to write about) their own personal encounters with the subject matter, and, to the extent they could function as participant-observers, those of their fellow students. In addition to their "field notes," they were to address these questions in a final essay: how and in what ways was this course different from college courses you have taken in other fields? What were the specific knowledge, skills and experience deficits you noticed in yourself (and in your fellow students) that got in the way of your mastery of the material? Excerpts from their field notes and final essays, edited for conciseness, are examined in later chapters of this report.

The study began with at least one assumption: the second tier is not the second rate.[18] So in the search for second tier stand-ins we looked for high achievers (in their respective fields) who were serious about their learning and career goals. We did not want our "tier" to be homogeneous since we believe that students who avoid science are most likely not homogeneous either. But we did want postgraduates with the necessary background to take college science courses. Our candidates were required to have taken four years each of high school mathematics and science, and one semester (at least) of college calculus. Such students, we believed, could, if motivated, successfully do science in college. Our hope was that these "surrogate students" would prove us right and at the same time help clarify the process and the problems involved in learning science.

To populate our program, we were looking primarily for mature postgraduates from fields as divergent as anthropology and creative writing. We found seven who met our qualifications, including one "fifth-year senior," and a college professor. Except for the classicist, none of our subjects had taken college science. Indeed, one had earned a kind of record for having enrolled in, and dropped, college chemistry more times than any other student in the history of her college (we placed her in introductory chemistry). The others had simply (and

---

[18] Some may object to the term "second tier" because it cannot help but imply "second rate." But I had committed myself to this term long before Richard Greenberg, a planetary scientist and chair of the University of Arizona's Interdisciplinary Committee on Teacher Preparation in Science, suggested a charming alternative, namely "osk," an acronym for "other smart kids."

successfully) avoided all science in college as undergraduates, yet had successfully completed bachelor's degrees in anthropology, philosophy, history, English literature, and creative writing.

We were looking intentionally for people who chose not to do science, not because they "couldn't" but because they had, in their own view, a "better" option. We found the seven to be confident both in their intellectual abilities and in their verbal skills, curious, hardworking, and efficient. Their maturity sometimes got in their way. They were, for one thing, more demanding and less patient with themselves and the material than their fellow students seemed to be. For another, they were more easily distracted by questions left hanging, and wondered about exceptions and applications. Their ability to observe their fellow students was clouded by overall disappointment in them. At one joint session (we met three times during the semester to exchange observations), we had to prohibit student-bashing just to get on with our discussion. Partly because they were graduate students and partly because the courses they selected were taught extremely well, they identified with their instructors and found them largely wasted on ungrateful, inattentive students. In many ways, then, they were not representative of "typical students who succeed in science" any more than they represented "typical students who fail." They were mainly themselves, learning a subject they had long ago abandoned, trying to answer questions for us and for themselves.

Our postgraduates were not (with one exception) much intimidated by the work. Sometimes they doubted their ability as when "the fellow sitting next to me was not taking any notes at all." But even where they succeeded, for some the excitement could not compensate for "the tedium." One subject remembered why she didn't take science in college. She had found high school science "too easy" and "not challenging enough." Several were shaken simply by the class size. It took the anthropologist days to adjust to being taught "out of a microphone." She felt it would not be possible for her (or anyone else) to ask questions in such a class and wondered if she would ever get used to it (she did). With one exception, all did very well in their courses. One subject tied for the highest grade in a (summer school) class. The others were easily among the top ten percent. But even with their successes, only two of the seven would continue in science if they had a choice. This is not necessarily because science is "hard," certainly not because they are "dumb," but, it could be argued, because they are "different."

The results of their semester-long encounters with introductory science (see *infra*) suggest that once we know more about students like these, we will have some clues as to why they prefer other fields and what strategies we can employ in college to woo them back. At the moment (except for our paid subjects) such students either don't show up in science at all, or are not present for long. Science faculty can only speculate on the possible causes of their disaffection. How much of the

16

distance such students put between themselves and science is the result of "inability," insufficient precollege mathematics and science, and college scuttlebutt about science? How much is due to the "classroom culture" of science, the environment and the style in which college science is taught?

If we are serious about recruiting new and different kinds of students to science, we need to know all this and more: how salient for them are financial and "lifestyle" considerations? How much of their migration out of (or unwillingness to try) college science is due to the demands science makes on their time? How much is due to the teaching of every science course as part of a professional apprenticeship and not for general utility or even pleasure? Most of all, we need to get to know these people, individually and as a group, and to listen to what they have to say.

The Second Tier Study

What follows is the beginning of such an effort. Eric Schocket was the first of the seven outsiders to science to be invited, with pay, to "seriously audit" undergraduate physics and chemistry, as representatives of an imagined "second tier." A summa cum laude graduate in literature from Berkeley, Eric was about to begin graduate study in literature at Stanford. He had entered college four-and-a-half years before with a strong mathematics interest and background, the full complement of high school science courses, and some motivation (but as it turned out not nearly enough) to do science in college.

In the summer of 1989 with the cooperation of a University of Arizona physics instructor and with Research Corporation support, Eric enrolled in an intensive summer-session course in introductory calculus-based physics—his first taste of physics since high school. He attended almost all classes during the five-week session, studied the text from three to six hours a night, handed in homework assignments, took quizzes and the final exam, all the while keeping a journal of his observations about the class and about his own personal encounter with the subject. He was instructed to notice in particular what made the course "hard" and even "distasteful" for the students in the class, and particularly for a special student like himself. Armed with a first-rate intellect, self-discipline and a record of successfully completing difficult courses in other fields, Eric did very well. Best of all, he discovered a liking for physical science, and averred at the end that if someone were to pay for his time, he might start over and do another B.A. in science.

In many respects, Eric is representative of the second tier. Had the sciences been made more attractive and accessible to him, had he thought his talents would be put to significant use in science, and had he been able to "try" science midway in his college career, he might have done science in college. But, except for some pressure from ROTC during his senior year in high school, Eric was not recruited to science either in college or before. Nor, despite his high school background, was he emboldened to try science as an elective. Eric had other options and developed "other loves" in college. Since he never appeared in a science course, no one in science ever got to know him (any more than he got to know them). As a result, there was no one, neither awesome professor nor friendly science teaching assistant nor science-trained college counselor available to him when, in the middle of his undergraduate career as an English major, he felt the need for more rigorous study outside of English. Observing that it was the treatment of *ideas* in literature and, especially in literary criticism, that attracted him to English more than the sheer aesthetic pleasures of poetry and fiction, Eric at one point considered a shift into philosophy. But he found philosophy, as currently practiced, narrower still, and so he stayed in English. Until recruited for this project, Eric never reconsidered science as a course of study or as a career. His journal and his postcourse reflections on the experience of taking college physics last summer give us insight into why.

Professional scientists may be tempted to dismiss comments and criticisms from second tier stand-ins as but further "proof" that they are not "one of us." But that would be missing the point. If the sciences are to attract any new group of students to science, either to meet the projected shortfall or to solve the science illiteracy problem, the effort must begin by getting to know some of "them," and well.

Introductory Physics: The Eric "Experiment"

"The notion of a 'calling' is deeply ingrained
in the mythology and history of science. If
we assume that all students are 'called' in
the same way and by the same age, we
fix what is inherently variable—
the size and composition of the talent pool."

—Daryl Chubin[1]

Eric found it "strange" to be in class again, especially in a lecture class where "everyone looks tired" and no one seemed particularly excited by the prospect of the five-week introductory physics course that lay ahead. His fellow classmates, as he perceived them, were either "bored" or "scared," he noted on the first page of the daily journal he was keeping of his reactions as a literature student to introductory physics. In even the most obscure literature class, he wrote, "there are always people who are intensely interested, at least at the outset. Is it simply the nature of the subject that makes elementary science classes appear unexciting, or is it the teaching style?"[2] Part of his assignment, as a participant-observer for a project supported by Research Corporation, was to find out.

Because it was a summer session, Eric would not experience the anonymity of the larger classes that characterize introductory physics. He shared his course with only 30 others, 20 men and ten women (not the gender balance he was used to, as he recorded in his journal). But the habit of teaching large classes and the demands of the fast-paced summer-school schedule prevented his instructor from modifying the lecture format. One look at the assignment sheets and at the weight of the text[3] gave Eric some sense of the amount of material to be covered, and some anxiety. To add to his travail, he discovered his calculator wouldn't handle exponents when he began to work the problems that first evening (he borrowed an HP 15-C the next day). More serious was his worry that, although he had taken college calculus (a condition of his assignment as participant observer in this course), his brain

---

[1] Daryl Chubin of the Office of Technology Assessment, U.S. Congress, made these remarks during a talk at the AAAS National Meeting, New Orleans, Feb. 17, 1990. Quoted with his permission.

[2] Eric, of course, was not around after class when the few students who were intensely interested in the subject went up to speak to the instructor.

[3] Halliday and Resnick, *Fundamentals of Physics*, Third Edition, New York: John Wiley, 1988.

wouldn't handle the computations. And it was clear there would be no respite either from the pace or the expectations. "The instructor gave the class the impression," Eric noted on the first day, "that since *he* had had to make it through the 'elementary grind,' so must we."[4] Literary studies offer a different kind of challenge, Eric noted right away. "In literature," he wrote, "the cutting edge is accessible, even if it is unlikely to be mastered by a beginner. In physics, a correct solution may be harder to figure out, but once done it will be indistinguishable from the professor's own." This insight soon became palpable for Eric when he discovered the "one nice thing" about physics: "as I try and endure, the understanding comes. And this does not necessarily happen in the humanities."

On the second day Eric began to notice more profound differences between the "values," as he put it, of a person in the humanities and those of a scientist.

> In a discussion of one of the homework problems, we were to judge the best clock for timekeeping, given a record of five clocks' readings at exactly noon. The professor chose the clock that gained exactly 51 seconds every day. I picked the clock that was within seven seconds of noon, day after day. A scientist wants predictability. I would rather have convenience.[5]

But the first "real day" of lecture disappointed him.

> The class consisted basically of problem solving and not of any interesting or inspiring exchange of ideas. The professor spent the first 15 minutes defining terms and apparently that was all the new information we were going to get on kinematics. Then he spent 50 minutes doing problems from chapter 1. He was not particularly good at explaining why he did what he did to solve the problems, nor did he have any real patience for people who wanted explanations.

Eric was learning that, for the most part, "why" questions are neither asked nor answered. The preference is for "how" questions. Perhaps because of this, his initial assessment of the teaching mode (compared to what he was used to) was negative.

> I do not feel that what this professor is doing can be considered teaching in any complex or complete sense. My understanding is that we are to learn primarily by reading the

---

[4] The instructor, reading these comments, did not recall ever using the term "elementary grind," but agreed that he brought to his teaching certain prejudices about who takes summer school physics and why: he assumed his students were "preprofessionals who have already decided on a career in science and are in class to learn problem solving." After reading these comments, he conceded he needed to be "more guarded about what I say..." and that "extreme care must be taken to set a good mood for the course, and to offset the prejudices students bring with them."

[5] Page 11 in the text, question 30P.

text, secondarily by doing problems on our own and comparing our solutions to those on sale in the physics office, and thirdly by mimicking the professor's problem-solving examples. Simply by intuition, I know physics, and more generally science, to involve creativity and finesse; but this man makes it into a craft, like cooking, where if someone follows the recipe, he or she will do well.

There was, indeed, a discrepancy between Eric's expectations and those of his professor (note 4).

By the end of the first week, classes seemed a little better or maybe, as Eric wondered, he was just getting "used to the way [the course] is being 'taught.'" Still, he felt patronized by the teaching style.

> I still get the feeling that unlike a humanities course, here the professor is the keeper of the information, the one who knows all the answers. This does little to propagate discussion or dissent. The professor does examples the "right way" and we are to mimic this as accurately as possible. Our opinions are not valued, especially since there is only one right answer, and at this level, usually only one [right] way to get it.

It was not the physics that bothered him. In later segments of his journal he would praise the text, a book borrowed from the physics undergraduate office that he begged to be able to keep when the course was over. He found his old love of math coming back. In the quiet of the university library where he spent afternoons trying to work the problems, he was "really quite content," he wrote. It was the class that bothered him most at the beginning, but he was honest enough to realize that as he "got more into the physics," he liked it better.

> As I am able to ask more knowledgeable questions, class becomes more interesting. I am finding that while the professor is happy to do example problems for the entire period, he will discuss the real world ramifications of a theory if asked.

His classmates didn't appreciate his interruptions, however. They seemed to "lose patience" with his "silly 'why' questions." These got in the way of the mechanics of finding the right solution to their assigned problems. And this was what, as Eric perceived it, physics was all about—for them.

He was finding more differences between doing physics and doing literary analysis. The professor's suggestion that setting up the problem and understanding concepts is more important than doing the arithmetic reduced Eric's homework time from six hours per night to three. He was happy to be relieved of some of the computation, but bothered, too. "Imagine being asked to show only that you *could* write a paper on the use of gender in *Tom Sawyer* without having actually to do so," he wrote in his journal that night.

21

Two weeks into the course, Eric was becoming skeptical about some of the models. His attention to language and his continuing need for answers to "why" questions was decidedly getting in his way. His July 9 entry reads:

> OK, I might as well admit it now. I don't really believe Newtonian mechanics. It works, yet somehow I think there are various forces which are made up—not really under-stood—just to make the calculations work out. Is there re-ally a normal force?[6] The force which pushes a book down on a table is gravity. Yet the "normal" force which com-prises the table pushing back on the book, seems a little strange. Why should a table push on a book? Maybe it should be called the "abnormal" force? And action-reaction seems to me to be a misnomer..."Action-reaction" presup-poses a cause and effect relationship which implies dura-tion, but in physics the "action-reaction" happens simulta-neously.[7]

By then he was starting to look around a bit more at the students in the class. Everyone looked clean cut and serious, he noted. Yet, there were a few people who caught his eye.

> There is one man with a crew cut who always sits in the front row and always wears a hat that says, "Life is too short to dance with ugly women." Another extremely mus-cular "frat boy type" catches my attention only because he always mutters the right answer several seconds before anyone else. I have decided he is either a genius or he has taken the course a few times before. There is a Hispanic woman who sits next to me who is already having trouble with the material. She tells me she spends seven hours a night on homework and needs to get an "A" to receive an ROTC scholarship for next year. A pretty blonde premed sits behind me. She acts like she wants to be friends, but her conversations always eventually turn to, "...By the way, what did you get on problem 57?"

Yet, even though the class was small, there was "no sense of commu-nity within the class," Eric noted, a fact he would later comment on at length. He attributed this to the lecture format and to the subject, devoid, as he put it, of "personal expression."

---

[6] Eric knew full well by then that the normal force in physics is the force perpendicular to the contact surface. He was playing with language.

[7] According to Arnold Arons, professor emeritus of physics, University of Washington, Eric's question concerning time intervals elapsing in connection with force adjustments having to do with Newton's third law, "is one of the deepest questions arising in classical physics. The question must be planted deliberately, and students must be led to think about and discuss it. There are very very few Erics who raise it spontaneously." (Personal communication to the author.)

Nobody seems particularly interested in making friends or seeing each other outside of class. This may be one reason people dislike math and science classes, their lack of community.

The first exam gave Eric some important insights both into how physics is taught and why the sense of community was so lacking. He personally found the exam "easy," easier than the homework which, as he expressed it, "involved the use of multiple concepts and numerical manipulations." In contrast, he wrote in his journal, "the exam problems asked only for a simple exhibition of skills acquired." He was "frustrated" to have spent so much time on problems which he would not encounter on tests. Later he concluded that the homework problems were really too hard, "discouraging rather than encouraging. Sometimes you are asked to display a knowledge of so many concepts at once, it is hard to get a hold of things."

But the real impact of the exam was felt when the exams were returned to the class.

> When we got our exams back this week, everyone was concerned about how other people scored. I understand that natural curiosity and in my literature classes there was always some comparing done between friends. However, I've never experienced the intense questioning that has happened this week. Almost everyone I talk to at some point or another asks me about my grade. When I respond I scored an "A,"[8] I get hostile and sometimes panicked looks. It is not until I explain that I'm only auditing and that my score certainly will not be figured into the curve, that these timid interrogators relax.

There was, in fact, no "grading on a curve" in Eric's course. The course handout had specifically stated this. Primed by other courses in science, students assumed they would be graded on a curve. The fact that the professor posted a histogram after each exam with the break points for the letter grades may have confused them. The professor said later, "maybe the students think a histogram implies a curve." His classmates' behavior, however, suggested to Eric that they fully believed grading was on a curve.

> It wasn't until this afternoon that a classmate explained to me that students in a science class try to identify people who score well and then constantly compare their scores (or time studying or answers on homework) to their own. I have never been in a class before where my grade had any effect, real or perceived, on anyone else.

---

[8] Eric did very well in the class. He never got the grade on his final exam but he averaged 92 during most of the course. See below for more of his comments about the examinations and the grading system used in his course.

Even more basic, for Eric, was the class' fixation on grades.

> Why is it so difficult to get a good grade? For one thing, there are less of them. Due to [perceived] curving in physics, the grades are based on the class average which kills any spirit of enjoyment. The message (though surely not intended) seems to be that no matter how hard you work—so long as everyone else works as hard or has more talent or experience—you *cannot* improve your grade.

Eric found the "sense of competition" in no way beneficial. "It automatically precludes any desire to work with or to help other people," he wrote. "Suddenly your classmates are your enemies." No wonder the class was not "fun," and there was so much hostility between students.

> My class is full of intellectual warriors who will some day hold jobs in technologically-based companies where they will be assigned to teams or groups in order to collectively work on projects. [But] these people will have had no training in working collectively. In fact, their experience will have taught them to fear cooperation, and that another person's intellectual achievement will be detrimental to their own.[9]

Still, he was impressed with his fellow students. Although the class continued to look "tired and bored" to him, he noticed that they "stick with it." He found there to be a "much more practical attitude about this class" than he had experienced in humanities. People think "yes, this is dull, but I have to complete this course to get my degree or to get a good job."

> In my literature classes it was much harder to rationalize this way. People took courses mainly because of interest in the topic or because they thought the professor would be good. It is not that a science course cannot be or isn't interesting, only that it's not required or expected by the students that it be so.

While some of the concepts were difficult for him and he continued to be bothered by the "constant qualifiers" such as "assume a frictionless surface," it was the pace of the course that he found "excessive, almost insane."[10]

> I usually give myself three hours for homework and never finish...I feel, though, that I have sufficient control of the subject matter [studying this way] to do well on the exams.

---

[9] The issue of teamwork is a centerpiece of modern science. See Daryl Chubin et al, *Interdisciplinary Analysis and Research,* Lomond, 1986.

[10] The professor himself admitted that the pace was "preposterous." Mindful that a summer school course is not typical, we continued the experiment with semester-long courses in the following fall. See *infra.*

Most of the other students I have talked to take six or seven hours a day to do the work...Aside from the pure misery of devoting that much of your life to physics, I wonder how much they, or rather we, will retain. I think that a slower pace and more in-depth discussions of the contents would, in the end, prove [more] beneficial.

He found the time demanded to be considerably more than he ever spent in literature—three hours per course hour in physics versus two hours per course hour in literature. Moreover, as he wrote during the third week, "physics homework demands a more intense, highly active type of thought."

Reading, however critically done, is a more reflective activity. There isn't the demand for almost instantaneous application of the information. The result of this difference is that two hours of physics is much more demanding and tiring than two hours even of [academic] reading.

The drawbacks of this amount of time spent may not be immediately apparent, he wrote. However,

with my extra time [as an undergraduate majoring in literature], I was able to pursue many different and independent types of educational experiences. Some of this included designing and running my own course, and [when an upperclassman] writing a grant-supported research paper. The science student is more often than not limited to the struggle of just completing required work.

When Eric asked himself, midway in the course, "what makes science hard?" he came to a preliminary conclusion that students will perceive a course to be "hard" when it is: 1) difficult to get a good grade; 2) time consuming; or 3) boring, dull, or simply not fun. Physics he found to be all of the above. But why introductory physics should be thought of as "dull" intrigued him. He kept coming back to the lack of community and the lecture format.

The lack of community, together with the lack of interchange between the professor and the students combines to produce a totally passive classroom experience...The best classes I had were classes in which I was constantly engaged, constantly questioning and pushing the limits of the subject and myself. The way this course is organized accounts for the lack of student involvement...The students are given premasticated information simply to mimic and apply to problems. Let them, rather, be exposed to conceptual problems, try to find solutions to them on their own, and then help them to understand the mistakes they make along the way.

But the concepts weren't easy and sometimes they didn't get cleared up at all.

> For some reason I am unable or secretly unwilling to com-
> plete these statics problems. Nothing seems to make sense
> and for the first time since my initial anxiety attack, I feel a
> cloud of bewilderment around my head...Tomorrow will
> give me a good opportunity, however, to see what venues
> are open to a student who is "lost." I will try buying a
> solution sheet and see if the problems make sense. If they
> still don't, I will go to office hours, an activity I've always
> hated. Someone who is clever will always get by; but what
> of someone who isn't? Is the measure of a course how much
> a bright student learns or how much someone who is "lost"
> can be made to comprehend?

Getting help was not easy for Eric or, he thought, for the others, despite the small size of the summer school class.

> If you find you do not understand something from the last
> chapter, you must wait until after class to see either the
> professor or the teaching assistant. The professor's office
> hour is busy and there is not much time for in-depth help.
> The teaching assistant, while well-meaning, has problems
> communicating in English, and is only around on certain
> days of the week. Even if you start to feel that you under-
> stand, you are faced with the task of the next chapter's
> homework, so you really can't afford the luxury of spend-
> ing yet another evening tackling the same problems.

As he lost some of his footing, Eric noted that it was much harder to "cram" for physics than for literature; hence it was not possible, as undergraduates are wont to do, to let the class "go" for a few days while he concentrated on something else.

The "best class" in Eric's view was one where the professor brought in five or six demonstrations, the results of which were counter-intuitive, and then asked the class to speculate as to why specific results occurred. In this class, there was substantial interchange. It led Eric to wonder whether a class could be designed that was "half lab, half lecture." But even more, he longed for study groups, arranged by the instructor for the class.

> The homework problems are hard and take an enormous
> amount of energy and patience. I think working together
> might engender an attitude that problems are enjoyable
> exercises...rather than aggravating stumbling blocks.

Worse yet, on any given day, the class worked on three separate chapters at once.

> Take June 13 for example. On this day, the professor an-
> swered questions on the homework problems from chapter
> 6, did some sample problems from chapter 7, gave us a quiz
> on the material from chapter 6, did some demonstrations
> pertaining to chapter 7, and began to lecture on chapter 8.

A consequence of the fact that students did their work "in private," Eric thought, was the absence of any opportunity for them to *talk* about the physics they were studying. They seemed inhibited, he observed, even about asking questions. Eric continued to do well on the exams and quizzes and was always surprised, even "shocked" at how low the class average tended to be.

> What this means is that there are a good many confused people sitting quietly and not asking questions. This is always the case to some extent in college, but physics seems harder on these people than the humanities. So much is based on what you should have learned the day before, that the course is a bit like a race where if you falter and don't immediately recover, you are sure to go down and be trampled.

The lack of "discussion" continued to fascinate and to bother Eric. He found that when he asked his classmates about what they were studying, they weren't able to "articulate an answer."

> I wonder if this is because they lack communication skills or because they haven't yet had the time to reflect on what they have learned, or perhaps because they don't really *know* much about their subject—if knowledge is defined to mean a deep, thoughtful understanding, rather than a superficial ability to regurgitate formulas.

One possible explanation might have been that in a course where answers are so critical, there is an inordinate fear of "making mistakes."

> One of the most frustrating things about the class is that the material comes so quickly. Once you stop "making mistakes" and master one chapter, you must move on right away to the next. Almost by definition, you wind up with more wrong answers than right ones. Learning physics becomes a process of making fewer and fewer mistakes, and moving on. There is no time to enjoy the success, no time to use those skills in order to discover more or dig deeper.

Still Eric was able to go deeper. He began to ponder the differences between mathematics and physics.

> Today I asked the professor why you figure *work* with a dot product. I got a different answer than I expected. Instead of talking about vectors and scalars, he talked about "what works." I realized that in physics, unlike math, you are much more concerned with getting real and usable figures than in the mathematical integrity of the operation. This is interesting because until this point, I did not really understand the difference between pure math and math as applied to science.

By the last week of class even the professor was "tired," or so he appeared to Eric. The class was but a shadow of what it had been. One-third of the students enrolled had either dropped out or were just not attending anymore. Eric noticed that the ratio of men to women, however, had remained about the same. The professor made numerous mistakes in explanation, and like everyone else, Eric thought, "just wants this class to be over." The "sudden shifts from particles to waves and then from waves to heat and temperature, without a pause, had everyone scrambling."

> There are no sad faces on this, the last day of class. No one will miss this chore. No one will say to himself or herself, "I really enjoyed that," or "that was an interesting learning experience." Instead, people will congratulate themselves on having made it, will be happy with their "B" or their "C," and will very soon forget anything pertaining to physics.[11]

For Eric, the final exam was a compressed version of everything that the course had and had not been, absent the "big picture." Eric had found all four exams in the class "biased toward computation and away from conceptual understanding." He understood that to be able to complete the computations required "some level of conceptual understanding." But that level was "not particularly high," he wrote.

> The problems [on exams] seldom required the use of more than one concept or physical principle. Only once were we asked to explain or comment on something rather than complete a calculation.

Eric thought the final, which was cumulative, would be the "... ideal place to tie things up and ask comparative and conceptual questions." Instead, he found that the questions entailed some fill-in-the-blanks definitions with terms found in a list. This caused him to reflect on the course more generally.

> We had marched through the chapters, doing the required work, but never digging deeper...I was able to keep myself on track by concentrating on one chapter at a time. But I never really got the idea that the professor had any understanding of how the concepts were related, as he rarely tied together information from more than one chapter. His lectures did not seem to build upon each other, and he gave no indication of a linear movement through a group of concepts...The final then asked the most primary basic questions about only the most important laws of physics. We were not required, at any time, to interrelate concepts or to try and understand the "bigger picture."

---

[11] Research by Hestenes et al confirms the failure of conventional physics instruction to overcome students' naive misconceptions about motion. Ibrahim Abou Halloun and David Hestenes, "The initial knowledge state of college physics students," and "Common sense concepts about motion," *Am. J. Phys.* 53 (11) Nov. 1985, p. 1043, ff.

It was not that the connective tissue was unavailable to the instructor; it was simply not featured. From the beginning of the course, Eric had liked the textbook and felt he had learned best from it. His ability to read through it on his own contributed to his early success in mastering the course. He noticed right away that the daily homework included an approximately equal number of two very different kinds of questions. One kind, for Eric, were only "exercises" and were assigned as homework problems. At one point in his journal he described these as "mathematical in nature and varying in difficulty from easy to nearly impossible." The second kind of questions were of a more "complex, conceptual nature." This latter kind interested Eric very much, but

> ...[since] these questions were never even mentioned by the instructor after the first day, nobody ever bothered to look at them. I feel that the professor misjudged the value of these questions and missed an opportunity to use them as launching points for discussions of the concepts.

After the final exam, Eric wrote that for him "the greatest stumbling block to understanding" was the lack of identifiable goals and the absence of linkage between concepts. He noted these deficiencies in answering a question we had posed: what makes science hard in general and for students like Eric coming to these disciplines as outsiders? He wrote:

> To some extent science is hard because it simply *is* hard. That is to say, the material to be learned involves a great many concepts, some of which are very counterintuitive. The process of mastering these concepts and being able to demonstrate a computational understanding of actual or theoretical situations requires a great deal of time and devotion. In my experience, this fact is well understood by the students, the professor and the general public. What is not as well understood are the various ways in which this already hard subject matter is made even harder and more frustrating by the pedagogy itself.

He feels that some "skeletal plan" would have helped him enormously to see how each individual property and theory is related to the "big picture." Comparing his introductory physics experience with that of the humanities, he wrote, "A professor who lectures on American literature of the 19th century might oversimplify the various social factors involved in each novel by referring to long-term historical events and trends, but at least his or her students would have some foundation on which to build impressions and judgments of the works."

The other "most difficult aspect" of the course for Eric was the "lack of student involvement" in lectures, and in discussion outside of class.

Simply being "talked *at*" suited this particular literature student not at all. He attributed his classmates' inability to articulate their subject matter directly to the fact that they got no practice "talking physics" in class.

Finally, he concluded, the "pressure involved in grade wars" goes much too far. He leaves us with the following advice:

> If one is truly interested in reforming physics education in particular and science education more generally, de-emphasizing numeric scales of achievement and rethinking the grading curve is certainly one place to start.

Discussion

The course we chose for Eric was a summer session version of the two-semester, calculus-based, introductory physics course which generally serves the "weeding out" role for chemistry, physics, engineering, and at some institutions, premedicine and biology.

The course is standard in its scope and sequence, so standard in fact, that four textbooks together dominate the postsecondary market. (One of them, the one Eric was to use, has more than a 60 percent market share.) Instructors justify their choice of one or another text based on the "quality" of problems and minor variations in the sequence of subject matter. Because it "serves" so many other fields, a course like Eric's will be taken by upwards of 100,000 American college and university students each year, of whom about 1,100 will go on to get the Ph.D. degree in physics. (Another 150,000 study the less rigorous, noncalculus-based introductory physics course.) One structural problem exists at the outset: the professor is training physicists; the students, for a variety of reasons, are taking physics.

When we had Eric's professor read what Eric had written about the course, this disparity was made very explicit. Eric's professor wrote:

> I assume that students in 103 are preprofessionals who have already decided on a career in science and are in class to learn problem-solving techniques that will be required of them in their careers...I [also] assume, however less and less, that the students have had some hands-on experience with how things work: clocks, cars, radios...and some experience with, and curiosity about, the physical or natural world. In other words, I assume I can make analogies to get across physical concepts. Students not interested in the physical world have a harder time, since they don't know, and usually don't care, how *things*, cars, bodies, weather, the heavens, work.[12]

---

[12] Personal communication from the professor to the author.

Eric complained that the "goals" of the course were never clearly articulated, and that the chapters were insufficiently "linked" or made to cohere. This was in part because of the fast pace of the summer session course, but also because the "unity of physics," assumed by the instructor was not explained often enough. Eric yearned for more "conceptual" information (we think he meant "interpretative"), and not just "facts" and the "mechanics" of problem solving. His professor was aiming his course at a different student. The teacher believed that, had he asked for any greater in-depth reasoning in class or on exams, there would have been "sheer panic."[13] In fact, he was adjusting his course to the needs and the limitations of the students he assumed he was teaching. Eric was asking for a different kind of adjustment, one directed to his intellectual curiosity.

According to Sharon Traweek, an anthropologist who studies the values, training and work styles of high energy physicists, Eric's complaints would not be perceived to be significant by professors whose goal is to train future physicists. From her interviews, she concludes:[14]

> [Successful] undergraduate physics students must display a high degree of intellectual skill, particularly in analogical [pattern finding] thinking. The students learn from textbooks whose interpretation of physics is not to be challenged; in fact it is not to be seen as interpretation. They learn to devalue past science because it is thought to provide no significant information about the current canon of physics, but they also learn from stories in their textbooks that there is a great gap between the heroes of science and their own limited capacities...
>
> [The emphasis on problem-solving is meant to] show students how to recognize that a new problem is like...familiar problems; in this introduction to the repertoire of soluble problems...the student is taught not induction or deduction but analogic thinking.

There are several ideas to be taken from the Eric experiment. Something besides the traditional problem-solving approach may be needed to excite *new* students to physics. But at least as important as content, if Eric's reactions are typical, will be changes in the "classroom culture" of physical science: more attention to an intellectual overview, more context (even history) in the presentation of physical models, less condescending pedagogy, differently challenging examinations, and, above all, more discussion, more "dissent" (even if artificially constructed), and more "community" in the classroom.

And what of the ten students who "disappeared" from Physics 103a

---

[13] *Ibid.*

[14] Sharon Traweek, *Beamtimes and Lifetimes, The World of High Energy Physics,* Cambridge: Harvard University Press, 1988, pp. 74 and 75.

last summer? Eric had no idea whether they had dropped the course or had simply stopped coming to class. In the "old days," a former chairman of the department told me, the course instructor would sign every course drop card, so there was opportunity for an "exit interview" and for some conversation about the course, the student's career goals and his or her alternate plans. Although Eric's professor did see a number of "drops" because of his advertised approachability, today drop-cards are handled bureaucratically by staff. Hence, there is less opportunity for retrieving the failing student or for soliciting students' views about particular courses.

If the science shortfall is to be stemmed at college, many more students should be made to feel welcome and valued, whatever their capacities and degree of commitment to science. The truth is science can be done by people who are not necessarily younger versions of their professors. Despite the emphasis in science on the "heroes" who contributed to what Thomas Kuhn calls "paradigm shifts" in the disciplines,[15] the scientific method was originally promoted by Francis Bacon precisely because it enabled "conventional minds" to do science.[16] Surely there is room in Kuhn's "normal science" for a larger portion of the college population than is currently made to feel deserving and comfortable in science. There is reason to believe many more undergraduates would respond to a differently constructed introductory course.

To an uncertain adolescent, flailing about for something he or she might actually be able to *do* and do well, science offers not just a whole array of interesting and important careers, but a training that, to paraphrase Bacon, enables ordinary people to do extraordinary things. If physicists learned to regard *every one* of those 250,000 introductory physics students—most of them somewhat better than "ordinary"—as having something valuable to contribute and much to gain from science, there might be no science "crisis" at all.

---

[15] Thomas Kuhn, *The Structure of Scientific Revolutions,* Chicago: University of Chicago Press, 1962.

[16] Francis Bacon, *The New Organon and Related Writings,* ed. Warhat, pp. 353-358, as quoted in Sharon Traweek, *op. cit.,* p. 80.

Jacki and Michele

The themes that emerged out of Eric's encounter with summer school physics were to surface again and again as the project continued. Mindful that summer school is extraordinarily fast-paced and that not all students would be as intellectual or as self-reflective as Eric, we developed a longer project in the fall of 1989 that would place six nonscience students as participant observers in semester-long introductory chemistry and physics courses. While the experiment did not consciously seek out the full range of potential second tier stand-ins, a somewhat diverse group of students responded to our invitation, among them Jacki Raphael and Michele Schoenfelt, graduate students in creative writing and philosophy, respectively.

Like Eric, Jacki and Michele had enrolled in and enjoyed science in high school but, for different reasons, had not pursued science at college. Yet, they rapidly forged ahead in their introductory physics course at the University of Arizona, demonstrating that above average intelligence and motivation, when combined with the power to reflect on what one is learning, contribute substantially to success in this field. While physics itself delighted and fascinated them, they found that the "logic of presentation" and the classroom culture still left much to be desired. The course in which we placed Jacki and Michele, Physics 111a, is an introductory calculus-based physics course, the first of a new four-semester sequence designed to capture potential physics majors immediately upon their arrival as freshmen. Normally, students interested in physics begin their freshman year with college calculus and only start physics in the spring. Fearful of losing them and of breaking the continuity of their high school-college sequence, the department of physics has created Physics 111-112 as an alternate physics sequence. In the first semester, the missing calculus concepts are taught along with mechanics; then three semesters (instead of two semesters) more are spent completing the introductory text.[1] Jacki's calculus skills were rusty but quickly came back. Michele was weaker in calculus and hence had more difficulty with the course.

Jacki

Her professor said of Jacki after she completed the first semester of Newtonian physics, "She could easily have been a physics major, and a

---

[1] Halliday and Resnick, *Fundamentals of Physics*, Third Edition, *op. cit.*

good one." Indeed, Jacki has the temperament of a scientist. She likes intellectual challenges and chose English over science as an undergraduate at Yale because science, as she thought about it then, was not sufficiently challenging. She brought to college a strong science background from a fine suburban high school in New Jersey. She had even, as she put it, been "programmed" to some extent to do science at Yale. But until we invited her to seriously audit Physics 111a at the university last fall, she had been a science avoider. She was enthusiastic about what lay ahead:

> I had good memories of high school chemistry and physics and imagined that, six years later, I would find college physics challenging and interesting. As a 24-year-old graduate student in creative writing, I was free from the career and grade concerns experienced by the average college freshman. I had the luxury to concentrate on satisfying my intellectual curiosity and, as I traveled, to reflect on my journey.

She used the term "journey" with its hint of magic because everything about the first physics lectures foreshadowed an intellectual adventure. She liked the fact that her professor was excited about teaching and about his subject. But, perhaps because she is trying to become a writer, she noted right away that her professor did not "narrate" his subject. He rarely told the students what they were doing or where they were headed. As a consequence, Jacki found herself faced with two disparate tasks: first, to understand the material being covered; second, to decide for herself how each part of the lesson fit in with the others. To accomplish this, she began to "construct my own narrative." She enjoyed the process but worried whether her narrative would correspond to the professor's. Like Eric, she was frustrated by a "missing overview," what physicist John Rigden, in amazing resonance with Jacki's own metaphor, calls the "story line."

> Why, I wanted to know, did we begin by studying only the idealized motion of particles in straight lines? What about the other kinds of motion? If he could tell us what's coming next, why we moved from projectile to circular motion, for example, I would find it easier to concentrate; I'd know what to focus on. In college, I always wanted to know how to connect the small parts of a large subject. In humanities classes, I searched for themes in novels, connections in history, and organizing principles in poetry.

How was she going to find connections in physics?

In time, she defined more precisely what she meant by "narrative:"

> In science in particular, teachers need to narrate with comments such as "what we didn't resolve last time" to let the

class know when it is plunging deeper into the material. [He needs to] show us how the subject is put together, its *grammar*...Not that you could not speak a foreign tongue without knowing the definition of a predicate. But in order to follow in lecture, I like to be told what I'm learning in terms of the language of the whole.

Apart from the missing story line, Jacki found the lectures extremely interesting and, at the beginning, the homework relatively easy to do if she put in the time. The course demands in general, she wrote in her journal, were "realistic and attainable with honest effort."

If you work the problems, you will most likely be able to solve them...That's what makes physics easy.

But, like Eric, Jacki was bothered by what she felt was an "exclusive" problem-solving focus. She noted that students put down their pencils when the professor discoursed on Aristotle, Galileo, and the history of science. They appeared to enjoy these excursions, but treated them as a kind of relief from having to concentrate so hard. Indeed, when she worked with the students in her study group, she realized that, as a rule, they did not want to talk about the problems conceptually.

Their concerns focused on the kinds of problems they would encounter on the exams, and not at all on a general understanding of the concepts...They ignored all the fun parts, seeing the whole picture, laying out the equations and solving these. Instead, they wanted to know what equalled what and solve for an answer. The elegance of problem solving was lost...

Jacki clearly had another agenda. After the second quiz, she wrote:

I wonder if I am different from the others...I don't care if I can solve standard physics problems easily. I want to get better at the tricky ones, the ones that ask me to use the concepts of physics.

Like the other second tier stand-ins Jacki was distracted by questions that were left unanswered, gleeful when she grasped, just before Thanksgiving, that "all along we were leaving things out in order to establish the basics and then move toward a fuller understanding of phenomena." And she was ecstatic when, toward the end of the semester, her professor paused and let her discover for herself why they had spent so much time "looking for laws of conservation." "Physicists," she finally figured out for herself, "want to locate permanence in change, the better to describe change." She guessed that most students in the class weren't "thinking much about such issues, but rather just writing notes, hoping they would absorb the material later." By mid-semester, she thought the students around her had become resigned to merely "taking dictation."

They have given up and don't even attempt any longer to follow the lecture. Not because the material is too complicated...I think theirs is a crisis of confidence and effort.

One day waiting in the professor's office while he "walked" a student through a particularly difficult homework problem, Jacki saw such a "crisis of confidence" on display. After struggling with a problem for a while, the student panicked and blurted out: "You can't put that on the exam. I'd never think of that!"

Jacki was not altogether free of anxiety herself. She was getting "A"s on her quizzes but described herself as quick to panic when insight didn't immediately come as she tackled new material. "Learning to solve physics problems," she would tell herself, "is a process, not a matter of insight." In her journal she attempted a definition of "understanding" as applied to physics. "Understanding the free-body diagrams means *knowing how to do them!*" But watching the professor do them was not enough. On a particular day, she noted:

When he goes through these problems the work seems so obvious, the equations so inevitable, that I tend not to question what he's doing...Lectures in physics can be incredibly passive experiences for students, particularly dangerous for those who believe [as Jacki sometimes did herself] that if they can follow the professor, they've mastered the material.

When she worked on her own, Jacki felt the "thrill" of understanding concepts and solving complicated problems. Yet, she found herself still resisting the *practice* required of her in physics. She speculated that it was not laziness, but rather

...the remnant of a prejudice of mine. Especially in the humanities, I value intelligence over technical mastery...I have come to see here that *intelligence is part craft.*

By the time the midsemester exam came around, Jacki was ready for much more than was forthcoming. Like Eric, she found the exam to be "nothing like the homework problems."

It was simple. It didn't really test understanding. There weren't elegant problems to solve. There were so many things I thought I was going to have to know that weren't on the exam: that normal forces are what a scale reads, the direction and nature of frictional force, that friction occurs toward the center of a circle against the bottom surface of the tires of a car rounding an unbanked curb, the difference between kinetic and static friction, what an inclined plane does to a free-fall, which angle is the bank angle, etc. I don't completely get all of this. But these are the questions I was thinking about when I prepared for the test.

These questions grew out of Jacki's "metathinking" about the problems she was trying to solve. It fascinated her that the two masses (inertial and gravitational) were independent of one another (within the scope of Newtonian mechanics); and that forces have regular, predictable components. "How organized the universe is!" she sighed one night into her journal. But she sensed that her fellow students were not able (or willing) to pursue such ideas.

> I think the students around me are having the same sort of thought-provoking questions about the material that I put into my journal, but under time pressure they don't pursue them, [and] eventually they learn to disregard "extraneous" thoughts and to stick only to the details of what they'll need to know for the exam. Since the only feedback we get is on the homework assignments, the students cannot help but conclude that their ability to solve problems is the only important goal of this class.

What would have served Jacki better was a more question-driven sequence.

> If a phenomenon acts on or affects two things, will the two be affected in the same way? This is the sort of question I like. I wish physics lessons could be presented as answers to such kinds of questions.

Also she wanted more time and space to speculate about the fundamental paradigms themselves. Once in a period of frustration trying to come to grips with the law of conservation of energy, she decided that it was so "artificial" as to be "bogus." "When energy is lost to friction, you have to include heat as energy to make the balance come out right," she wrote, and this bothered her. Later, she got her professor to explain to her privately that

> ...mechanical energy is really just part of the physicist's way of explaining conservation, a way of freezing a system at a moment of time, a descriptive tool, but not a tangible amount of energy per se...I really liked this. I felt I was learning something very important about physics. I don't mind if formulas are used to describe strange, unknowable quantities, or relations that are necessary merely for consistency. Language is such a system, philosophy for sure. I like that aspect of physics. I just want to be certain I can see why and how physicists describe the world.

Because Jacki's math confidence was high and her calculus skills rusty but still in place, she was able to stand back from the computations and contemplate the *relation* between physics and mathematics. When one day, working two simultaneous equations, her professor advised the class to try squaring both equations to eliminate one variable, Jacki was fascinated that an algebraic manipulation would "work" in physics. She knew that "you can't understand the physical world not knowing math," but wondered more profoundly, "how math is intrinsically related to the physical world."

Her appetite for the overview was finally being satisfied, if only by the questions that "distracted" her and by the narrative she was constructing. Toward the end of the course, she could chronicle her own progress.

> When we first did physics problems we ignored certain variables: friction, heat, and the pulleys over which cords ran with masses on the ends. Problems with parts such as inclined planes were idealized to be smooth, frictionless, simple. As the semester progressed, we gained the technical means to quantify friction, how to take the rotation of a pulley into account. Now we can study the effects of forces in more detail. We can describe the decelerations of a billiard ball, for example, after it has been set in motion and until it comes to rest. Things that used to be simple in our problems are complex.

But why didn't her professor "tell us this was how we would progress? Why did he wait to the end?" One answer might be that, in science, students cannot understand where they are headed until they get there. But the frustration for Jacki was real and made her, like Eric, feel much like a child.

> I never really knew where we were heading or how much, in the real scheme of things, we had already covered. Each topic the professor discusses feels like it's being pulled out of a hat. So the general feeling I was left with was that physics was endless, that there would always be one more complex way of describing motion...I was made to feel too much like a naive child, whose parent tells me one small thing at a time, making everything seem equally mysterious.

Part of this was the "ownership" issue that Eric had felt, too. Jacki liked and admired her professor but felt she could not share in the "intimacy" of his relationship with physics.

> *He* knows the whole picture, how to solve complicated problems, even to talk philosophically about the problems and the issues of physics. *We* have but a fraction of that intimacy. There are whole areas we know nothing about. We don't even know these subtopics exist. That's how ignorant we are. His goal may be to get us to understand physics the way he does [but] his method, inevitably, is that of a grade-school teacher because we are like grade-school kids.

In contrast to her humanities classes, where

> ...you're encouraged to think on your own. Sure, the professor gives you background material and provides the details you will need to know to analyze the subject. But the *ap-*

proach is what is being studied. You can disagree with your professor's approach. And the moment you begin thinking *about* what the professor is saying, you're on your way to developing your own unique relationship to the material. The way we think about physics is not an issue in class. We don't know enough. The best we can hope for is learning something about how the professor thinks about physics.

In the end, Jacki was not enthusiastic enough about physics to let it change her life. She did agree to take the second half of physics 111, hoping it might rekindle that initial "spirit of adventure" she had looked forward to in early fall. She felt, on balance, that physics was presented as a "race to get control of a specialized knowledge," and that "this striving for mastery" made physics not the *intellectual experience* she had hoped it would be.

Michele

Michele Schoenfelt was a first-year graduate student in philosophy when she agreed to audit Physics 111a. She had begun college with a strong interest in science, but except for introductory astronomy, she had taken none—this, despite the fact that in high school she had been primarily a science student in the advanced math and science track at a good, large public school. "Back then I took virtually no humanities classes and all the science I could get my hands on," she wrote in her journal. This included one year of physics, two years of chemistry, and two-and-a-half years of biology. She had mathematics through trigonometry and was, beginning in her sophomore year, a lab assistant for biology and chemistry. As she remembers, she did very well in her science classes, enjoyed them immensely and even participated in the Physics Olympics. Leaving high school, she fully expected to earn an advanced degree in "something like organic chemistry."

What dissuaded Michele was a combination of events: a freshman's reluctance to take classes that, as she remembers, "all started at 8 a.m.," and a number of "discouraging experiences."

> One of my counselors had started out in biochemistry and warned me that a lab was a very lonely place to work. The introductory astronomy class which I had expected to love turned out to be quite bad. It was a lab only in name. The professor used the weekly hour of lab time to make us do nothing but computations on paper. He had promised we would be allowed to use the observatory; he never lived up to that promise.

Instead, during her freshman year, she began a lifetime "love affair" with philosophy.

Like Jacki and the others, Michele was enthusiastic about the opportunity to take physical science for the first time. She brought to the subject a true curiosity about the physical world and an expertise in those branches of philosophy that would be particularly relevant to her work as an observer: logic and epistemology. Like the others, she attended classes, did homework assignments and took two of the four hour exams that preceded the final. Then, instead of preparing for the final, she polished up her journal and wrote for us a reflective essay on her experience.

Unlike Jacki, Michele found the mathematics very difficult (she was not as well prepared), and that it "intruded" on her search for mastery of "concepts." But the content was not as difficult for Michele as it was "demanding:"

> I spent more time doing physics than I did working on any one of my graduate-level classes in philosophy. There was always homework, even on the day an exam was scheduled. Homework problems were supposed to take about 15 minutes, but they usually required much more time. Review sessions and exams were piled on top of class hours, i.e. scheduled out of class time. You really have to be committed to a subject to be willing to devote that much time to it, semester after semester.

She also experienced "discouragement" caused by failure to master the next level of problems quickly and easily. But, as a philosopher, she was able to reflect on the experience. Science, she noted, demands that one not be discouraged by failure:

> In solving problems you are expected to make many mistakes. By the time you eliminate your mistakes you're off to a different type of problem...This causes enthusiasm to wane.

Like Eric, she was bothered by the lack of "creativity" demanded of her and by what she thought was a requirement for excessive conformity.

> Science demands that you do your work the way the instructor does. It allows [at this stage] for precious little interpretation. This is as it must be, but if you don't like this, it can be difficult to force yourself to conform.

But most of all, Michele fretted over the dominance of the quantitative.

> My curiosity simply did not extend to the quantitative solution. I just didn't care to figure out how much. I was more interested in the "why" and the "how." I wanted verbal explanations with formulae and computations only as a secondary aid. Becoming capable at problem solving was not a major goal of mine. But it was the major goal of the course.

As a student and sometime teacher of philosophy, Michele was very able to grasp what bothered Eric about the lack of "explanations." She found herself "obsessed," as she put it, with gaining a "discursive understanding" of a concept before using it. But she was more willing than Eric to acknowledge that "sometimes you have to accept procedures just because they *work*." She began to appreciate that "understanding comes with practice," but still found herself spending a lot of time "banging her head against the wall." Her physics course demanded more patience than she was very often able to deliver. Moreover, as Vicki was to conclude (see *infra*), the way the course was taught did not play to her strengths.

> Science demands that you work in an orderly fashion. If you're accustomed (as I am) to solving problems by using shortcuts and doing as much as possible on the calculator without writing things down, you get into trouble...

Besides the demands made on students, Michele found a number of things which "in combination" were alienating. She listed these as:

> Too little time allotted to simply reading the text. This reinforces the message that doing problems is all that is called for.

> A course design that assumes that everyone in the class has already decided to be a physicist and wants to be *trained*, not *educated*, in the subject.

> The absence of a "road map," and the feeling that "curiosity questions" have no place in class discussions.

> Too easy exams in contrast to too hard homework. On philosophy exams, Michelle noted, instructors expect their students to do more than what they've done before, not less.

Contributing to her sense of frustration was the homework schedule. Homework assigned at the beginning of one class was due at the beginning of the next. As a result, she noted, there was no chance to ask questions in class about the homework before turning it in. And after it was turned in, little motive to ask questions about difficult problems or to strive to understand them even if they were explained. Michele thought a larger set of problems, given at the beginning of one class and due two classes later, could have promoted greater class interaction, and more effort expended on difficult problems.

Michele was acutely aware that physics required her to reverse her usual method of learning. "Performance," she wrote, "comes before competence." She understood that many concepts in science are best grasped via manipulation and experimentation. But she found this "performance first, competence later" sequence capable of paralyzing, or at least considerably frustrating, certain students who would say, if they could articulate their problem, "I can't use it unless I understand it, and you tell me I have to use it in order to understand it."

Beyond her desire to learn concepts more "discursively," Michele did not find physics concepts particularly difficult to master compared to abstract ideas in other fields. But she did offer some insights into why some intelligent students may decide to leave science:

> If creative, innovative students are to be retained in greater numbers, instructors are going to have to...give them more of a sense that they are not just walking down the same trodden path of problem after problem to solve. Students need to know the goals, the structure, and the way science and mathematics relate [so that they can exercise] their curiosity and critical thinking powers.

Discussion

As the preceding amply demonstrates, Jacki and Michele were quite capable of grasping the scope and purpose of their physics course. But this in no way reduced their impatience with the emphasis on problem solving. As Michele put it, there were too many "how much" questions, not enough discussion of "how" or "why." Individual problems intrigued and, on occasion, even delighted all of our second tier stand-ins, but only when they led to understanding and did not merely test skills. For several of our auditors, and as Tom Worthen would write in his journal (see *infra*), the problems were of limited interest because they had "all been solved before."[2] Only occasionally did these exercises provide intellectual satisfaction; rarely were they a source of new insight. Our auditors mastered physics problem solving as well as most of their peers (with the exception of Vicki; see *infra*). But they looked upon the effort, almost without exception, to be *training* at the expense of *education* in science; too many scales, not enough music.

For their professors on the other hand, *proficiency* at problem solving is more than a disembodied skill. It is the essence of their subject and of their pedagogy, the very core of the introductory course. Instructors in physical science who teach beginners believe that problem solving contributes to at least three of their teaching goals: 1) imparting the basics of the subject (Newton's laws, atomic and molecular theory, the periodic table); 2) explaining how physicists or chemists make sense of natural phenomena—how they think and what they do; and, 3) preparing students who continue in science for what lies ahead. To do all of this most efficiently, they focus on the quantitative nature of the concepts. So the concepts of force, field, valence and oxidation states,

---

[2] Physicist John Rigden of the American Institute of Physics, quoted before, says that many of the brightest physics majors are bothered by this as well.

molarity and chemical equilibria are presented not as "words" or "ideas" not even as "explanations," but rather as embedded in techniques.

This goes far to explain why our auditors perceived their courses to be low on "concepts," even on "theory," and why they felt mired in "facts." (Jacki at one point called these "dry formulas" and "dull reality.") Michele came closest to speaking for all when she characterized herself as "not impressed" by the fact that something works (a formula or a model) unless she was given, in addition, a "discursive understanding of the idea." Perhaps what we have here is not so much a disagreement about content as a problem of communication. The second tier stand-ins felt that the "formulas came too fast." They wanted more time to wrap their own intelligence and intuition (their "creativity") around exploratory questions; to be given the formula or the explanation only later when they had exhausted their own imagination; and to learn the appropriate technique as a *means* toward solving problems, not as an *end* in itself. As Tom noted, to take but one example from chemistry (see *infra*), more attention was given to Avogadro's number (merely a conversion factor from atomic mass units to grams) than to Avogadro's insight! A typical complaint.

A difference between our stand-ins and many of their fellow students was their skepticism about models. Eric had problems accepting the idea that constrained motion has to be understood in terms of forces. For a while Jacki regarded the law of conservation of energy as "bogus." Michele marveled that the physicist's model of reality could be so "unreal." That something works (a formula or a model) was not sufficiently persuasive. Had their professors time for some history of physics, they might have better understood why these models work. Eric eventually became comfortable with the notion that any environment, including any constraint on an object in motion, has to be described in terms of a set of forces. Jacki finally understood, profoundly, that the law of conservation of energy is defined so as *never to fail*.

Professors encourage these insights. Indeed, they reveal them to students all the time. But they teach as if these insights will emerge naturally from the experience of setting up quantitative problems and solving them, perhaps because this is the way they were taught or because this works for them. While for many students this is the way understanding comes, for Eric, Jacki, and Michele it was patronizing not to be told in advance where they were headed, or what they needed to know to understand. That's why the experience conjured up for Jacki the image of herself as a naive child whose parents tell her one small thing at a time and keep the whole mysterious.

The challenge for the teacher of beginning physical science is to teach techniques, along with the sophisticated concepts that underlie the techniques, without either patronizing students or cheating them of the creative and critical thinking that science also entails.

In Pursuit of Chemistry:
Tom, Laura and Stephanie

"There has to be room in science
for people who did not ask for
a chemistry set at age five."

—Harry Ungar[1]

Nearly 2,500 students take introductory chemistry at the University
of Arizona each year but the yield, in terms of chemistry majors, is only
about 20 per graduating class. The department does not have a recruitment strategy. In the opinion of one of its senior members, students
who major in science (or engineering) will have made this choice years
before entering college, and the department believes it has neither the
right nor that it would be effective to try to "seduce" students into
changing their career plans. The large enrollments result from requirements in fields other than chemistry. Among these are engineering,
agriculture, nursing, premedicine and the like.

To accommodate large numbers of students with diverse interests
and backgrounds, the chemistry department offers three levels of introductory courses: honors chemistry for students who have had advanced physical science and mathematics in high school (at least half of
whom are headed toward engineering)[;2] Chem 103, the standard college-level introductory chemistry course for all science, engineering
and premed majors,[3] and Chem 101, a slower-paced, less quantitative
course which attracts prenursing and nonscience majors, among others.[4] Chem 101 and 103 are so populous that their instructors are each
responsible for two different sections of 250 students. This means they
each lecture six times a week and supervise the work of 500 students.

Apart from the students already interested in the major then, chemistry does not manage to attract many newcomers to the field. This is
not to say that the courses are not "good" or well taught. To compensate for the enormous class sizes, the department goes out of its way to

---

[1] Harry Ungar teaches chemistry at Cabrillo Community College, Aptos, Calif. (personal
communication to the author).

[2] Textbook: T. Moeller, J.C. Bailar, Jr., J. Kleinberg, C.O. Guss, M. E. Castellion, and C. Metz,
Chemistry With Inorganic Qualitative Analysis, Third Edition, New York: Harcourt Brace,
1989.

[3] Textbook: R. Chang, *Chemistry*, Third Edition, New York: Random House, 1987.

[4] Textbook: F. A. Bettelheim and J. March, *Introduction to General, Organic, and Biochemistry*,
2nd Ed. New York: W.B. Saunders, 1988.

assign master teachers to the introductory courses. Since Chem 101 and Chem 103 enroll a great many students not headed for the chemistry major, we were pleased when we found three second tier stand-ins so that we could have auditors in both courses.

Unlike physics where we selected auditors and then enrolled them in introductory courses, the chemistry candidates rather fell into our net. Tom Worthen, a professor of classics, was on the verge of taking general chemistry anyway and was too interesting a "case" not to use. Laura Fulginiti, a graduate student in physical anthropology, had already enrolled in Chem 101 on her adviser's suggestion that it would make her a "well-rounded anatomist." (He had no way of knowing that she had started and then dropped undergraduate chemistry for years.) Stephanie Lipscomb, a 1989 graduate of Smith College in history, had begun what she hoped would be a postgraduate premedicine program for which she needed chemistry and biology. Each of our auditors had taken science in high school and, except for Worthen who had started out as a science major in college, each had also taken some college mathematics but no college science. Because they were of superior intelligence and motivation once we briefed them on the nature and purpose of our study, we expected good insights from them about chemistry.

Tom Worthen

Tom Worthen might have become a scientist had he not "hit the wall," as he put it, 30 years earlier as a Caltech freshman. Coming to that western "shark tank" from a less competitive high school environment in Utah, Worthen's successful background in high school science and mathematics turned out to be inadequate to the Caltech challenge. He left Caltech after one year, and returned, defeated, to Utah. After a break, his mathematical interests were redirected to ancient languages. In time he received the Ph.D. in Greek and Latin and became a professor of classical languages and history at the University of Arizona.

In midlife, Tom Worthen became interested again in the math-science subjects he had rejected or, as he would put it, that had rejected him, so many years before. As a serious auditor, he studied college calculus at the university in the summers of 1987 and 1988. When in September 1989 he responded to our advertisement seeking second tier stand-ins, he named general chemistry as his subject of choice. Thus, he found himself enrolled along with 250 other students in a section of Chem 103. Like Eric, his expectations were high. He had, after all, been reading *about* science for many years and has a penetrating, demanding mind. But like Eric in physics, he was not expecting the almost exclusive emphasis on problem solving. Of the first few weeks of introductory chemistry he wrote:

The lecture system as practiced in this large course has, I believe, some pedagogical shortcomings...I hear remarks that this stuff is too easy, "we learned this in high school." I have a feeling that those students who have so far been coasting through the work on units, stoichiometry and heats of formation, are going to have difficulty when we get to energy levels and the application of Planck's constant.

Nonetheless, I think that their comments are not without basis. The professor takes 90 percent of class time solving problems which are illustrative of concepts treated cursorily, as if the concepts were the entrée to the problem set instead of the problems being drill for the concept...The emphasis is, has to be, on the right answer appearing underlined somewhere on the page. True, there are appealing procedures, but this does not correct the basic message that *accountancy* is what doing well at chemistry is all about...

Also, like Eric, Tom Worthen had an appetite for "concepts:"

It would be better not to waste the expertise of the professor on working problems hour after uncomfortable hour. We need to know more of the background of Dalton's laws in ancient atomic theory and of the work done on gas laws during the 18th century. As chemistry students we should know the evolution of Avogadro's concept from the point at which he conceived it up to the determination of the size of the constant named after him. The periodic table, how it was intuited, filled in, and gave clues to the understanding of the electron configuration of atoms, is a subject which ought to be covered in depth. These fascinating subjects would keep our budding chemists from being bored with last year's problem solving.

As he proceeded through the course, his initial impressions were not altered. The problem sets were definitely the "core of the course," and in time Tom found them "interesting and even fun." But like Eric, Tom found the examinations to be "over basic materials," requiring only "the memorization of formulas and values of constants." Worse yet there were "no new conceptual challenges" for Tom on the exams.[5]

Still, the lectures remained for him the "weakest" part of the course. Not that the professor did not know his material or how to present it, but his approach,

...probably set by department policy, was to recapitulate the textbook and work sample problems...It was difficult to sit

---

[5] Commenting on this observation, Tom's professor said: "The purpose of an examination in chemistry, in my opinion, is to allow the student to demonstrate that he or she has mastered the assigned material. No tricks, no curve balls, no red herrings. A 50-minute examination is a power test. There is no time for reflection, contemplation or creative thinking. That's why we give the problem sets [to] provide students with the opportunity to reflect on the work and to discuss the problems with their friends."

there for an hour of this without participating. And participation was definitely not encouraged. When it happened, it very often led to chaos. The class was much too large to allow everyone to ask questions.

In addition to the lack of participation, he felt the lack "of inspiration, of an overview of the goals of the course or the science of chemistry, glimpses of how this subject and knowledge of it can make me a better citizen of my nation, of the world—a better householder."

> I would much rather be asked to attend a formal, inspirational lecture once every week or two and spend the rest of my time with a TA or a Macintosh solving sample problems. There would be at least some degree of interaction with a machine. We spend much too much time gaining technical knowledge of chemistry, necessary to be sure, but there is formal and even informal information which could be presented to us without numbers and details whereby we might learn what chemistry is doing on the cutting edge, what are its various subfields, and more of its history.

Tom soon understood the driving force behind the lecture: the presentation of *all* the material. Yet he found the text (Chang) so excellent and well laid out that he thought a bright student could easily get through the course "with just Chang in hand and the professor's problem sets in the other." Why then was time spent going over the textbook material in class? In the end, he found himself doing so well in the course that he was tutoring students who were taking it along with him. More impressively, he wrote for *himself* that "overview" that he had wanted to hear from the lecturer. Perhaps if the lectures had offered the kind of introduction to "thinking about chemistry" Tom Worthen had to develop for himself, a greater variety of students would have done better in the subject and, more important, would have liked it more.

Once Tom had a grasp of what *he* thought was the "essence of chemistry," he had some thoughts about why students trained in subjects like classics and history would have difficulty.

> Modern chemistry is an extremely complicated subject. Its study requires the mathematics and especially the concepts of physics, including quantum mechanics, even at the beginning level where the nature of matter is the subject of discussion. So one must be part mathematician and part physicist to study chemistry. Then one must gain an instinctive feel for the periodic table, at least in its first five periods. This is a "touchy-feely" sort of skill like learning the keyboard of a typewriter. You come to a knowledge of which element goes in which column and in which row. Without that skill, the kinships among the elements remain a mystery even with the table in front of you. Then there are the "whys" of the periodic table, learning electron configura-

tions with their quantum numbers. [The] combination of elements with each other or with others to form molecules requires a different but interrelated conceptualization. The logic lies in the pattern.

Science is science—measurement and counting--and this means units, formulas and constants, and one must memorize these and understand why one is required to do so. But memorization is not enough. One must understand the dimensions of a formula, why it has those dimensions and how those dimensions reflect the principles of nature. A historian's mind will not suffice for a scientist. The historian's mind is like a library catalog; the scientist's mind is like a computer programmed to logical analysis. One doesn't discuss science except at its cutting edge. All one can do with history is discuss it.

Tom was slowly moving away from one comfortable learning strategy and trying to grasp another.

But grasping the "essence of chemistry" was not going to get Tom through the course. He had homework problems to prepare once a week, and quizzes and exams to take. Like other students he wanted to do well and was frustrated by a grading system that prevented him from being properly assessed. He was well prepared for the first exam:

Here's Hess's law, molarity, understanding of relationships between mass and moles of isotopes and elements. Empirical formulas, stock system, balancing of equations with calculation of reagent amounts. I thought this exam fairly easy but very fair. A good test of principles involving a minimum of calculation. Horror set in when I got back a 87!

After consideration, Tom decided that his paper had drawn "a tired or poor grader."

My method of calculating percentage mass to percentage mole was not done the way the grader expected. I was docked for not giving units when I had expressed my intention to convert mass to moles; then there were significant figure errors in calculating an empirical formula. Why does one need significant figures in an empirical formula when one is looking only for near integers?

Tom appealed his grade and got a 98, wondering how many potential premeds had been washed out by the same kind of grading, and why, if there was no "curve," the class average was always pretty close to 70. Tom thought the professor had stated at the beginning of the course that while he didn't grade on a curve, he had a point system "which experience has shown will yield the proper distribution of seven percent 'A's, 18 percent 'B's..."[6] By the end of the fourth week,

---

[6] The course actually was graded on a curve.

judging from class attendance, Tom figured 15 to 20 percent of the class had dropped out. As a professor in a much less populous field, he felt some envy for the chemist's "leverage."

> The kids, when they appear here, do so out of fear. Their careers are on the line, and a good grade in chemistry is a must for a premed, a chem engineer, a chemist. My students [in classical languages and literature] are tourists. Turn up the heat and they head north fast.

As a "student," Tom began to develop a useful and usable problem-solving strategy, using intuition and working "backwards." One night, on problem set three, he reworked a problem involving hot lead and cool water four different times and got four different answers.

> Finally, I decided that the only way to solve the problem was to estimate the answer from formal intuition and then find the math that would give an answer near that ballpark figure. This I did by noticing that the values I had been subtracting before, if added instead, would give my guesstimate. This was the right answer, but I still don't know where I went wrong with the signs. I felt like a drunk trying to figure out which way to get on the freeway.

Tom finally realized he had forgotten to change the sign of the change in temperature when transposed across the "equals" sign. On the next problem he saved two-and-a-half hours by realizing that since water was the only substance involved, all the specific heats would cancel out. "Intuition first, intelligence second," he remarked. Later he found that

> ...instead of merely solving the problem, I found myself playing with the conditions. The grader liked my little game and commented on it. Maybe I'm getting into science. I wonder if it's too late to change careers!

He learned also to memorize the most general formulas, laws and constants and then derive the specific corollary formulas needed for a given problem as the occasion arises. Something was working, he wrote. He was getting 98s on his problem sets.

Moreover, he was finding that the problems supplied the "participation" he was missing in class.

> One *participates* with the mind of the person who sets the problem. It's...like reading sophisticated...literature. It takes some training to get anything out of it at all, and the greater the depth of experience, the more you see in it.

He began to do so well on problem sets and examinations that his papers were "ripped off" by other students, a common occurrence, his professor told him. He did not know whether to be angry or flattered.

Like our other auditors, Tom was asked to observe his classmates' attitudes and behaviors. In the aggregate he found them to be "rude," and even speculated that "courses like this inculcate rude behavior in students."

> Half the kids are eating or drinking something...The place looks like a movie theater after the show when they leave, cups and papers scattered about. There is a constant coming and going during the hour which increases exponentially as the hour approaches its end. The students shut their books and begin to pick up belongings at 2:47 regardless of what the prof is trying to say, or how he is trying to conclude. Often he just gives up and lamely says, amidst the clamor of their departure, "Well, I guess that's it for the day."

A contributing factor, surely, was the "lack of community" in class that all our auditors commented upon. Tom sensed that no connections were being forged among the students.

But Tom could and did make contact with individuals through his position as resident adviser in a women's dormitory. When his "charges" heard he was taking introductory chemistry, they sought him out.

> One of my dormitory charges came to me for help last evening. I looked at her notes...Formulas without units, figures running here and there like an early Greek inscription. Fill all the available space. Design the page, but there was no clarity on her paper, nor in her head.

Tom's intellect and curiosity often caused him to spend more time than was necessary working on a section of the course. Once he worked until 1 a.m. churning through material on molecular orbital theory.

> It is fascinating material, but it has complicated tables to lay out each new isotope from hydrogen through lithium as each new proton and neutron are added to the periodic table predicting the existence of such an entity and its properties, if it could exist as a stable element.

When he went to the professor for help, he was told that the material was "entirely inappropriate for chemistry at this level" and would therefore not be on the exam. Instead of thinking the three hours wasted as an ordinary student might, Tom was pleased to have finally arrived at something he thought of as "cutting edge" chemistry. He was even more pleased when, toward the end of the course, his professor privately offered Tom his "last law in chemistry," namely that all science is tentative.

> In discussing the forces contributing to lattice energy, we learn [in principle] that since the attractive forces are directly proportional to the charge and inversely as the square of the distance between them, small ions with large charge like magnesium should form high bond energies. But the curve is not flat, so I asked about it. As a general principle

50

this is good, I said, but does it not apply across the board? "Nothing works across the board in chemistry," my professor told me. "Large atoms are 'squishy' and there is some covalent energy in the bonding, so the lattice energy theory accounts for only 70-80 percent of the bonding energy."

Perhaps the "historian's mind" Worthen had previously thought inappropriate might be of use in chemistry. The classics scholar had arrived in science.

Laura

Laura Fulginiti was a fifth-year graduate student in physical anthropology. She had enrolled in and dropped college chemistry more times than anyone else in the history of her school, possibly as many as seven times. She had no fear of mathematics, and mastered college-level calculus and biology even though these were not required for her major. In recent years, she has specialized in gross anatomy, a "back door," as she puts it, into medicine. So what we had in Laura was not a science-avoider per se, but someone for whom science had to be made particularly appealing and nonthreatening for her to be able to succeed. Chem 101, the "safer," slower, introductory course, was the access point to science she chose for herself. Most likely other members of the second tier were there as well.

Laura's training in anthropology made her a particularly good observer. And her first impressions of Chem 101 reveal those skills. She decided to keep changing her seat in class so that she could better observe a wide range of student behavior.

> The first day of class I opted to sit in the back section so that I could get a bird's-eye view of the room. The professor wears a microphone which creates a distance between himself and the class. It was a new and disturbing experience for me. Students wander in late. There is lots of rustling and whispering. A woman two down from me is painting her nails. The attitude of the students seems already ingrained. Those who do not expect to succeed are already not trying.

Later, she observed, as had the other auditors, that the students "seem to watch the professor for clues as to what is important."

> They key into buzzwords and catch phrases. They write down whatever he puts on the board, but not what he says in lecture...People listen for what they think they have to know. They are not turned on by ideas.

Like the other auditors, she noticed how attendance diminished and how passive the students were who came to class.

What was it about the first few lectures that made people drop [or stop coming to class]? Were they bored because they had heard it all before, or were they overwhelmed? Difficult to know...I marvel at the professor's ability to ignore people sleeping in front of him. Whether it's his fault or not, there is just no excitement in this class.

She also commented on the focus on exams.

Everybody including the professor is geared towards exams. He'll say, "You don't need to learn this. It won't be on the exam." While this provides moments of welcome relief and apparently fits in with his overall game plan, it reinforces the already exam-directed behavior of the students.

As it turned out, the disappearing students did not drop the course. They simply stopped coming to lectures, for, as Laura noticed, "attendance swelled again on exam days."

Laura had no difficulties with either the course's text, its pace or the examinations. But, like our other auditors, she commented at length on her disappointment that the scope of the course didn't include theory, interpretation, or what she called "creative thought." While she wondered at times whether she wasn't placing unwarranted demands on introductory chemistry, she noted that introductory anthropology, a freshman course she was coincidentally auditing at the same time, managed better to integrate fact and "metafact."

Chemistry is a very hard and fast science. Facts are facts and at the introductory level there is little debate about what is presented to students. Basically, there is a body of information that has to pass from professor to student and there is no room for interpretation or creative thought. There is, in the final analysis, only one right answer, and all others will "generate red marks" as our professor likes to say.

I found myself craving some theory, some discussion of how the laws of nature were developed, rather than just being presented with the finished project...In introductory anthropology, theory is presented along with the "basic dogma" of physical anthropology. The professor brings articles to class that refer to what is happening on the forefront of molecular biology and shows how it fits in with what we are studying. Although the [cutting-edge] material is somewhat overwhelming and difficult to understand at times, it adds a dimension...that is missing from chemistry.

A high point in Chem 101 for Laura and, she thought, for her classmates as well, was the professor's discussion of the accident at Chernobyl. But even here, the treatment was

[digressive], not the focus of our work, not material with which students can creatively interact.

The key issue for Laura was "motivation." Overall she found the material not too difficult. She enjoyed her growing ability to solve problems, and mastered what had first been difficult for her to do, namely memorize details and formulas. Of herself and of students like her, she wrote the following at the end of her journal:

> Students, properly motivated, can learn this stuff with little difficulty. [But] students have to feel confident to stay interested. Four exams plus a final may serve to motivate students to "keep up," but the constant assessment can also erode confidence. Professors are going to have to rethink their strategies, along with their priorities, if students like me are going to be attracted early on, when it really counts, to science.

Stephanie

Like most female high school students, Stephanie Lipscomb was not encouraged to pursue science in college. She doesn't remember being "openly discouraged," but

> ...I was certainly not given the belief that I could give something to science and that it could give something back to me.

A girl friend, more predisposed than Stephanie to science, gave it up at Yale, because she found that the only people who took science there were the ones who were "really good at it." Another friend succeeded in science, Stephanie thinks in retrospect, because she studied at an all-women's college.

Yet, Stephanie could have become a science major. With the exception of chemistry, her experiences with science courses in high school were positive. She did particularly well in biology and physics, with teachers, she remembers, who made the courses both "challenging and fun." But chemistry gave her difficulty.

> The equations, atomic structures and the periodic table mostly mystified me. They were more difficult to make sense of, to visualize, than the anatomic structures of biology and the projectiles of physics. I distinctly remember my chemistry teacher telling me at one point that I lacked "common sense" in chemistry. I wondered then, and wonder still, what that meant.

Instead of pursuing physics or biology, Stephanie went to an eastern women's college which had no core requirements, and graduated with honors and a B.A. in American studies in May 1989. At Smith she didn't take a single science course. "I was learning other ways to think and liking it a whole lot," she wrote. But upon graduation, without any immediate employment plans, Stephanie began to think of medicine as a career. And so, in the fall of 1989, she enrolled in introductory physics, biology and Chem 103, committing herself to a total of nine lectures and three, three-hour weekly labs. Three weeks into the semester she dropped introductory physics because it was proving to be the most time-consuming of her courses, with a problem set and a quiz to write every week. She also was opposed to the way physics was being taught.

> The problem sets and quizzes were written in a highly impersonal format. The students answered the questions by filling in one of three circles, "A," "B," or "C," for machine grading. But the answers were not multiple choice. Instead, students had to work out the problems and choose "A," "B," or "C" based on the first significant figure of their answers.

It didn't take Stephanie long to realize that a student's answer in physics could be off by an order of magnitude (2,200 m/s, for example, instead of a right answer of 257.34 m/s) and still receive credit. Furthermore,

> since the answer sheets are posted in the hallway a week later, it is a lot to assume that the student will take the time to compare his answers to those on the answer sheet and to detect (and learn from) mistakes which the computer failed to pick up in the first place.

So, although she believed chemistry would be even more "difficult" for her than physics given her past history, she remained in Chem 103 and let physics go. She spent the rest of the semester attending all but one of the lectures in Chem 103, completing all problem sets and taking all four exams for credit, even though midway through the semester she decided, for the second time in her life, not to pursue science or medicine. She decided there was a "mismatch."

> I process information in a different way than it is taught or utilized in science courses. I learn to understand by putting [concepts] into my own language, not by memorizing and spitting out the words as I received them. [Also] the humanities and social sciences seem to be *patient* with people like me...Science seems to hurry off before I get too close. It avoids my attempts to touch or shape it.

She didn't know whether her fellow students were experiencing the same difficulties, but she did notice that they "did not, for the most part, take an active role in the learning process."

> [They were not] attentively taking notes, computing problems along with the professor, or asking questions. Most appeared bored. Either they had the material before, or they were totally lost. It was hard to tell which.

Most of the material struck Stephanie as "dry, factual, and rule-ordered." And it seemed to her she must "plod through the rules to get to anything more interesting."

> ...There is nothing really stimulating about balancing equations, or determining heats of formation, nothing that makes us want to raise our hands and say, "wait a minute, that's a pretty groovy reaction. Would you go over it again, so I really understand why it works that way?"

She felt, looking around, that most of her fellow students "couldn't care less" unless something was going to be on the exam.

> The equation has no meaning unless they need to know it for the exam. We are only told the rules in introductory chemistry: hydrogen bonds with highly electronegative oxygen, nitrogen, or fluorine. Period. "You'll need to know this for the exam." Or, "don't worry about this. You won't need to know it unless you get into higher chemistry."

Rarely did the professor allow the subject matter to come alive for Stephanie. Rarely did he move above or beyond the basic rules. She was grateful that he made things "manageable," and that there were "simple, easily memorized ways to approach the material if all else fails."

> So we memorize the pattern and perform the electron configuration problems correctly on the exam. But what do we really take with us after the exam is over? What will we have learned?

The professor, Stephanie correctly guessed, "knows the material is dull, so he allows it to be dull." In commenting later on her journal entry (as he did on all the auditors'), Stephanie's professor agreed, but explained that it has to be that way. He wrote back to the author:

> It is dull. It is dull to learn, and it is dull to teach. Unfortunately, it is the basic nuts and bolts stuff that must be mastered before anything useful can be accomplished...I guarantee that if we changed our course and eliminated the admittedly boring...stuff, most departments now requiring a year or more of chemistry would no longer do so. They would teach the nuts and bolts stuff themselves. I think we can do it better.

For Stephanie the course was "dull" not because of nuts and bolts, but because,

> ...as the recipient of this [predigested] information, I am not stimulated to *think* all this information through, as I copy it into my notes. So, when a question or doubt arises in mind, I let it float on by...

The times Stephanie learned best were when the professor actually demonstrated a chemical concept.

I remember the styrofoam models and [really understood] crystallization by watching it actually take place. Gas diffusion, too, [came alive] by seeing the pressure increase on a homemade gauge. It was useful to grasp how temperature relates to gas density with hot air ballooning and, as an example, why people are more successful ballooning in the winter rather than in summer.

But sometimes during lecture the rhythm was "too comfortable," and like the other students Stephanie would lapse into "automatic pilot." It was too easy for her to "synch and sink" as she put it in her notes, and just write down what the professor said while allowing her mind to wander.

In times like these, I wondered how many of the other students were turning away from chemistry, even if it meant turning away from medical school. And there wasn't a whole lot that would bring them back.

Although she gives her professor high marks for presentation, some days she found his tone mildly patronizing as when, during a discussion of atomic structure, he pointed out that students could think of covalent bonds as an "idea" shared between two atoms. Stephanie followed his train of thought eagerly until he quipped, "If you want to think about it deeply, which I don't think any of you do..." She "instantly recoiled," offended by his remark. As an older student, Stephanie appreciated that "remarks like these" were doubtless due to the relentlessness of the teaching process and the absence of a *relationship* between teacher and student. In her final essay, she wrote:

Not sure whether the professor's teaching methods are the *cause* or the *effect* of the "collective ennui" of the class.

Other times, she noticed that

the professor tiptoes toward a particularly interesting explanation of a chemical concept, something to take us above and beyond the basic facts, only to tiptoe back again.

Stephanie wanted more, for example, on Heisenberg's uncertainty principle. She saw it as a missed opportunity to "talk some theory, to analyze the limits of measurement itself and to move into a realm beyond the basic cut-and-dried facts." She recognized that this was precisely the sort of discussion that would stimulate her to learn, even to enjoy, chemistry.

But almost as quickly as [the professor] moved into this area of discussion, he skirted right back out again, reluctant, I suppose, to get bogged down in material we weren't really interested in or didn't need to know for the exam.

In the end Stephanie's most satisfying learning occurred in the tutor room (Arizona's is one of the few chemistry departments to provide this service). During the semester eight problem sets were assigned, each consisting of five or six detailed problems on the material covered to that point. The professor encouraged students to work together in groups, explaining to them that "in the real world most of the problems are solved by group effort." But Stephanie never figured out how, in a lecture hall of 250, she was supposed to pick out the people with whom she could do these problems, until she discovered the tutor room. When she got 32 points out of a possible 34 on a problem set thanks to the tutor room, she knew what it was to "feel great" about chemistry.

> I would go in, sit down at one of the three tables with some other people I didn't know, and pretty soon we would all be discussing the material and working the problems together. Whenever we were stumped, we could bring one of the tutors over to the table to help us out. It was a very good system. Here we had a solid block of time [for Stephanie, three to four hours] to interact with other students, work problems, discuss and actively learn the material we were covering in lecture.

Stephanie's method for studying for exams was not as effective, she wrote later, as it was "comfortable." She would read through her notes and refer to the text whenever she felt she needed a more thorough understanding. Then she wrote up a study guide of her own design, based on the notes and the study sheet passed out in class. The rewriting process, she thinks, afforded her not only the necessary review but also an occasion for restructuring the material.

Still, or perhaps because of her study methods, she received only average scores on exams throughout the semester. Looking back she thinks it was because she tended to become "impatient" in areas where she could manage only a "surface understanding." Hess's law and calculating heats of reaction were two of these.

Further, she was reluctant, until the last two exams, to thoroughly memorize the names and formulas of compounds. Sometimes these sections were worth 15 points which, she remembers ruefully, "put a sizeable dent" in her final grade. But her main problem was not unlike Vicki Pike's (see *infra*):

> I wasn't willing to change the study habits and thought processes which had worked so well for me in literature, history and political science...I insisted on studying to understand, not memorize and perform. To get higher scores on the exams...I needed to solve a wider variety of problems...

Despite her mediocre performance on the tests, Stephanie began to feel "comfortable" with chemistry, both with the material and with the "pace of it all." She enjoyed her labs particularly because they gave her a sense of the "practical applications" of chemistry. Indeed, in lab she frequently found what was missing in lecture, namely an opportunity to "speculate beyond the simple chemical properties to the implications of the experiment itself." After a while, even in lecture, she was getting to the point where

> ...I could let it come to me, and I would absorb it, understand it, even enjoy it, without having to force it down...It didn't taste so bad when I relaxed and stopped worrying about grades or the exams.

Still, the objectives of Chem 103 remained ambiguous and the course, in some fundamental ways, disappointing.

> What was I supposed to be learning in chemistry? A way to look at the subject? Do the problems correctly? Become analytical? And what were the professor's goals? Did he wish us to succeed? Was I to be an inheritor of a vast, multifaceted science? Or just a technician?...In the humanities and social sciences we are taught to ask "why" questions. In chemistry I felt we were only being taught to ask "how." How certain chemicals behave when mixed, how we find the limiting reagent in a reaction, how we derive the molar mass from *amu*. If we didn't know "how" we surely couldn't pass the exams. [I felt that] those of us who prefer "why" questions do not survive in this course. It has no use for us, no patience with us, and we are pushed away.

If introductory chemistry was a "weeding out" course, it succeeded, Stephanie wrote at the end of her final essay, because it weeded her out. But she was not clear whether "chemistry had no use for me, or I no use for it."

> I came away from the course feeling that turning kids on to chemistry was not a goal [of Chem 103], and that only [committed science students] would succeed. I was weeded out because I didn't like the impersonality and the size of the class, because I wasn't as motivated as others to "ace" exams, because the material never really captivated or stimulated me in ways that I am used to being stimulated. [For instance] I never really gave the subject much thought after class. Perhaps I needed to adapt to the ways of science in order to adopt it into my life.

Whatever the reasons, science is losing some valuable minds, and one of them was Stephanie's.

Postscript

In reading Tom Worthen's and Stephanie Lipscomb's observations, Laura Fulginiti was struck by how similar the experiences were for all three, although they were taking different courses. Chemistry, she feels, is the culprit, not the particular course sequences or the pedagogy that might distinguish one introductory approach from another. The absence of history and context, "the tyranny of technique," the isolation of the learner and the struggle to attend in a sea of inattentiveness—these were issues not even the best instructors (and chemistry offers its beginning students its very best) could overcome.

The Herschbach Approach[7]

In 1987 in a remarkable (but of course entirely coincidental) "response" to our auditors' complaints about introductory chemistry, Dudley Herschbach, professor of chemistry at Harvard University, introduced what he calls the "grand reform" of Chem 10, Harvard's upper-level introductory course. He describes the course changes as follows:

On the first day of class, Herschbach gives his students a philosophical lecture on the "nature of science," making the point that science is extremely amenable to the human psyche; that truth is "waiting patiently at the top of a mountain for us [him and his students] to achieve it. The only question and challenge is how to get there." The theme of his message to students is that it is more important to be "ardent" and "persistent" than to be "brilliant." Moreover, it is neither necessary nor desirable to be "right" at every step along the way. "People," he tells his students who are unsure about science, "are like enzyme molecules, floating around, groping to find something they are destined to catalyze." In this way he tries to get his students to believe "you won't know whether science is or is not for you unless you stay around and give it and yourself a chance." For the first time in his working life as a teacher, Herschbach is not giving a text assignment and a problem set the first day of class.

To set a different "mood" for the students in Chem 10 and to deal with the "anomie" and competitiveness of this typical introductory chemistry course, Herschbach has initiated some unusual innovations: he plays music (their music) as students walk into class, and meets with an elected "student advisory committee" every other week for continuous feedback as to how the course is going and how the students feel about it. In addition, he makes himself available at one of the Harvard-Radcliffe dining halls once a week for conversation with whichever students appear. They talk informally and he listens to what they have to say about the course (and anything else on their minds).

---

[7] Taken from a talk given by Dudley Herschbach on the subject of his revisions of Harvard's introductory course in chemistry at the National Meeting of the American Association for the Advancement of Science, New Orleans, Feb. 17, 1990. My rendering of the talk, as written here, has been read and approved by Prof. Herschbach.

All this is meant to "humanize" introductory chemistry, but at least as important in his view has been his decision to try the Rigden strategy: "cover less and uncover more." He uses parables (narratives) to reinforce the information, frequently refers to applications, and focuses on the qualitative (as against the quantitative) approach to solving problems. He requires his students on their problem sets to *think* about problems qualitatively before plugging in numbers, even (especially) to "guess" at answers in advance of doing the work. He believes that "unless they have a qualitative understanding of the problems they are doing, they will have trouble handling any variant of a problem in their homework and on exams." Just because they have the right answer, it doesn't mean they have the right *idea* about the problem. He is, in his words, "forcing them to *think*."

As regards grading, Herschbach offers two unusual gifts to his students: first, as he announces on the first day of class, students will not be allowed to compete with each other, i.e. Chem 10 will not be graded on a curve. He wants them to compete with a standard he, their professor, has defined, and if they do so successfully, all of them can get "A"s in the course. Second, and even more innovative, is his idea of "resurrection points." Any points not earned on a particular hour exam or quiz can be "resurrected," made up, on the final. The system works as follows. The points a student misses on a particular hour exam, the student's "unearned points," are "book-kept" on his or her individual record in such a way that the corresponding section of the final is *absolutely* increased in value by that same number of points. So, if a student scores 90/150 on the first hour exam, then the first part of the final for that student will be worth 100+(150-90)=160 points. The second part of that student's final might be worth 120 points, the third part 140 points, and so on.

Final exams then, in Herschbach's Chem 10, are individualized to account for previous difficulty and to *reward* compensatory work done by students between the hour exam and the final. This is what Professor Herschbach means when he tells the class at the beginning of the semester: "You are not allowed to lose any points [permanently] on an hour exam!" For students this translates into the possibility that, however poorly they performed prior to the final, they always have the opportunity to "ace" the course.

The "grand reform" of Chem 10 has only been in place three years, but several outcomes have already been observed.

One effect, a large increase in enrollment in the course, occurred even before the first cycle began in 1987. As usual Herschbach had appeared prior to the beginning of the semester at a special orientation meeting for freshmen "interested in science." At this meeting he announced two of the innovations: absolute grading and the "resurrection" points. That first semester, class enrollment nearly doubled, from 170 in the previous year the class was taught, to 300. Herschbach and his colleagues attributed this increase directly to the "news about grading." Previously, many students who had qualified for Chem 10 (on the basis of AP courses or their scores on a qualifying exam) had opted, instead, for the lower level introductory course, put off by Chem 10's reputation for being "cut-throat."

Despite the near doubling in enrollment, the students in Chem 10 have on average performed better than their predecessors. This has been documented both by their (absolute) final grades and by their teaching assistants' impressions. (A number of chemistry TAs teach two years in a row at Harvard.) Morale is noticeably better, and as for persistence in the major, Herschbach reports that enrollment in chemistry at the junior level (physical chemistry, the first course in the standard sequence for majors only) has reversed its previous decline and is on the rise.

Dudley Herschbach's pedagogical innovations in chemistry are grounded in his own personal philosophy about "who does science, and *when*." Herschbach believes there are (at least) two kinds of science students: those he calls "sprinters," students who are quick to grasp new material and who do very well at the kind of manipulations demanded of them in introductory science, and those he calls "long-distance runners," students who may appear to move more slowly and with greater difficulty, but whose grasp in time is profound. Science, as it is currently taught and evaluated in college, Herschbach believes, favors sprinters over long-distance runners, a significant loss to science, he says, because the latter, if they persist, often make the most important contributions.[8]

---

[8] Dudley Herschbach's assessment of the impact of the "grand reform" in Chem 10 and this last statement of his personal philosophy as to who does science and when, are from a personal communication from Prof. Herschbach to the author.

Physics Revisited: Vicki

"The course did not play to my strengths"

Vicki Pike was not a sprinter. More than any of our other second tier stand-ins, she had difficulty in the introductory physics course at the University of Nebraska in which we placed her as yet another participant observer. She had considerable strengths in learning in general, and much experience in studying and studying well. But the material did not come easy and when she applied her "tried and true" methods of studying social science to the task of mastering physical concepts, she found they didn't "work." Two things stand out as she writes about her valiant struggle to master the first semester of physics. First, how little even hard and sustained study could compensate for her missing (or underused) mathematics skills and the problem-solving strategies that are appropriate to mathematics and physics; second, how similar to Eric's, Jacki's, and Michele's were her responses to her physics course, despite her poorer showing. Vicki found much in physics to excite her. She believes to this day that with some kind of sustained prephysics preparation she would have done better. So while Vicki most likely would not have become a science professional, greater science literacy was well within her grasp.

Vicki Pike was a fifth-year senior majoring in anthropology at the University of Nebraska when she agreed to seriously audit introductory physics there. While science had once been "an option" for her, she had not pursued it in college. Like so many state university students, Vicki had always needed paid work (as much as 20 hours per week) while going to school. For years she had worked at jobs that usually did not, as so often is the case, relate in any way to what she was doing in college. So she was very pleased to have a paid assignment that would take her into a classroom where she could learn something she had only brushed by during her four years in college. At the same time, she could practice her participant-observation skills, skills she had developed as a student of anthropology. As it turned out, Vicki was to add significantly to our understanding of what makes introductory physics difficult and even alienating for a substantial minority of students. She was our "average" student and gave us certain insights that would not otherwise have been forthcoming.

Placed in the standard calculus-based introductory physics course at Nebraska, Vicki found herself with 70 other students, most of them engineers. "In addition there were," she reported, "an astronomy major, a geologist, a meteorologist, and me." Her "minority" status, then, was threefold. She was a social science major, a paid participant-observer, and a woman. Although her professor reported later that three of the women students in that class earned "A"s in the course, by midsemester some of the seven females in the class had begun to "cluster."

At first, more than any of the others in our sample, Vicki was discouraged by the course in physics. At the outset this had less to do with the physics itself (that came later) than with the fact that she was receiving poor grades on homework and short exams. Like the typical college student, Vicki had got in the habit of judging herself by her grade-point average, and when she found it difficult (as it turned out, impossible) to win honor grades in physics, she was frustrated and resentful. She found the exams to be not a "true measure of what I am learning." She had particular trouble with timed tests. "Tests and quizzes in this course," she complained, "work to my disadvantage." The competition and the time limits "discredit what I can do."

> Why can't I have the time I need to show what I know?[1] That's not what they're measuring. They're trying to find out how I do in relation to others...Then, when I get a really poor grade, I feel awful, even though I am not taking the course for credit...It took me a month and a half [nearly half the semester] to get over that feeling.

Like Eric, she was put off by the "classroom culture" of introductory physics. She recognized that the "attitude of the discipline" was being imparted, along with the physics, and conceded that it was probably necessary to do that. Her professor, meaning well, talked much about Nobel prize winners, and men (mostly men) who had been "first" in their discoveries. While he said later that he described many different models of scientific work, he admitted that "telling is not teaching," and what Vicki picked up was what she called the "Newton model," i.e. the scientist working alone. Even though her professor encouraged his students to work in study groups and Vicki herself eventually found two people to study with, she took away from her hours of lecture the sense that "sharing," as she put it, is not "highly valued" in this culture, and "not sharing" is tolerated in ways that she found unusual.

There was little *evidence* of group work in the recitation section where students competed with one another, or in the biographies of career scientists sketched out in her text. Since Vicki was previously socialized in another discipline where, as she put it, "learning is done through discussion with other students and with the professor," she found it demoralizing to be working alone, in isolation, in a culture she

---

[1] Vicki might have benefitted from an alternative grading model, one that does allow the student to "show what I know." See "The Herschbach Approach," p. 59.

characterized as destructively competitive: "I have the answer. Do you? If you don't, I'm not going to share it with you." She also found the physics classroom to be "hierarchical." She didn't "want to know where I stood vis-à-vis every other person in the room." And she didn't like it.

Vicki actually enjoyed the lectures and the recitation sections, but was confused as to their role and purpose in this particular course. She got a great deal, or thought she was getting a great deal, out of the information imparted by her instructors, but began to suspect, midway through the course, that the other students had an entirely different strategy from her own and that theirs worked better.

> Some people seemed to go to class only to hand in their homework...Others would attend lectures purposefully to get information in order to digest it later, and in private. I wanted to digest it there, in class, through questions and discussion. I learn verbally. I like being put on the spot. I am not passive as they seemed to me to be.

What she may have been saying is that she wasn't used to struggling with this type of difficult material on her own. But there were other issues, among them differences between her approach to lectures and that of her fellow students. Her fellow students, it seemed to her, wanted "just the facts" as if discussion would "dilute and confuse." Her note-taking, in contrast, was significantly more laborious than theirs. She would write study sheets for herself during and after class, trying to re-explain the material in language she could understand (a technique that, incidentally, works very well for students outside of science). Her notes were full of words. Her fellow students would just "write equations."

One can easily explain these differences. They are typical of the classroom cultures of science and nonscience courses. What might have helped Vicki would have been some training in note-taking or, better still, some unsolicited advice from the students sitting on either side of her. But they were not generous.

> People act differently in physics. The seating arrangement militates against being social, integrated. There are lots of atomized individuals with desks placed between them. Physics is not a place where people befriend one another.[2]

Intellectually, Vicki remarked that she was unable to cope with what she described as "text and derivations without *explanation* [italics added] of what it all means." It is significant that what her professor

---

[2] Upon reading this, Vicki's professor remarked that this had been a particularly unfriendly, even "hostile" class, made up of students who didn't want to be there. Many of Vicki's classmates were as afraid of physics as she, and their passivity in class may well have reflected that. While Vicki sought help outside of class, she never came to either of her instructors for assistance. Her second-tier assignment may have been the inhibitor.

and her recitation instructor thought they were doing to *explain* the difficult material, (describing physical phenomena in terms of the laws of physics), didn't *feel* like an explanation to Vicki. And because her grasp of calculus was uncertain (she had taken calculus for the first time two years before), she found herself taking an inordinate amount of time to do her homework and she was never on top of her exams. By mid-November, she was not passing the course and she was bitter. Had she been a truly average student, not part of a paid experiment, there is no question that Vicki would have dropped the course and never attempted the physical sciences again. But she was obliged to stay and to monitor herself learning physics, and so she did.

In time, Vicki found an acquaintance, a computer science major outside the course, who offered to help her. But those sessions made her feel still more "different," even disabled. She wrote:

> It seemed to me the whole time we were working, our wires would get crossed. He would say "We need to find the velocity." Then I would ask, "why?" It was not obvious to me...But then we would move through the problem and I would see that velocity was needed for the formula that would produce the results we were looking for...His logic seemed backwards to me. I wanted to start with a formula which would be *concrete* [italics added] and then find what was missing...He was so used to these problems, it was obvious to him what steps to take. He was not very sympathetic to my needs and my lack of experience.

Her "logic" was not only "backwards," her learning strategies failed her, too.

> When he brought up an equation, I would try to relate it to another equation to help me learn them both all the better. This confused the effort. When John works a problem he uses only what is necessary and brings nothing else into the process. If I am going to learn a subject I need to know what is similar and dissimilar about an item. Why, when you are pushing down on a moving block, is there no "work" done? Isn't there a force downward on the block? I know that force and displacement have to be in the same direction; I needed to relate this to the concepts in the problem...John seemed disturbed by this and thought I had not yet mastered the "elementals."

On another occasion, her difference in approach to physics was made even more clear. This time she had two study partners, Mike and Tom.

> That afternoon I studied with Mike and Tom. I was there early and was reading through the chapters trying to get a hold on the concepts. I figured that was the important part. If I can apply the concepts, I can look for the formulas I

need. When Mike and Tom arrived, the focal point shifted to solving problems. I was still more concerned with studying the text. Mike said, "You're too worried about the concept...Let's just do the problem." This really bothered me. Aren't they integral parts? How could I work a problem without understanding the concepts that underlie it?

After thinking about her friends' "problem orientation," Vicki realized that she had been wrongly concentrating on the text and lectures and not "practicing" problems. Indeed, her "interest in concepts" was actually distracting her from problem solving. For her problems were a "test of understanding," not a "key to understanding" as they were for many of the others. She attributed this mainly to lack of experience. That "study mentality" which she had brought with her from success in other courses was not serving her well in physics. What Vicki had been looking for were things to *compare* to one another, and for *context*. And she had not known where to look for these in physics. It is not that there are no comparisons or contexts in physics. It is simply that these were not highlighted or made palpable for her. She vowed to change her "habits" if she could. "What a great time to figure this out," she wrote in her journal, "just before the second exam."

Vicki had been asked to observe not just her own encounters with physics, but the attitudes and behaviors of the other students in her class. She was fascinated by the fluctuation in attendance. When she asked him midway through the course, her professor assured her that 70 students were enrolled. But the average attendance was between 40 and 55 and sometimes as few as 30. "How do the other students survive," she wondered, "without coming to lectures?" In courses in the social sciences where the curriculum is nonstandard, lectures are more critical in that they define the scope of the subject and provide interpretation. In physics, she began to note in her journal, other aspects of the course mattered as much or more.

> No one ever asks questions in class except for that rare "Will you clarify?" question. I feel like it is grab-and-run. Perhaps physics is so straightforward that it can be taught without interaction, but a part of it, I think, is that the students seize the opportunity to be anonymous.

On another day, when she was more excited about what she was learning, Vicki wondered why there was no buzz; why, as she put it, "no one besides the professor and those destined to be professors ever gets excited about the material."

> I know most of the people here are required to be here, but don't they ever try to find something redeeming about the class? I hear only negative comments, even that the course is called locally "Phy-sucks." Even the people who do have the ability [Vicki had concluded by then that she did not have it] turn away.

Vicki eventually found that her best studying came while working with at least one other student, "teaching the material to one another." Here she was able to do what she could not do in class: question and try out what she thought she understood, and then question again. "I must be a 'high activity' learner," she concluded. There was just not enough "activity" for her in the lecture and discussion sessions in physics. (We did not have her take labs, so it is conceivable she would have found the "activity" she was missing there.) Keeping up remained her major problem along with being too slow in solving problems on exams. She found it particularly difficult to be "at one place in lecture, at another place in recitation section, and at still another place in my mastery of the material." She hated being "forced to hand over my unfinished examination paper when I have stretched my time to the limit." She saw this as a real threat both to her grade and to herself. "The others must have felt, as I did, that if we could just sit and think for a while, we could figure it out."

Toward the end of the course Vicki was enjoying physics and learning much more than her grade point average revealed. Her journal is filled with references to the physics itself and to her appreciation. "What is nice [in translational and rotational motion] is that everything seems analogous to what we have learned before. There are just more variables now to worry about." Conservation of angular momentum came alive for her, as it does for many students, when she was asked to think about why a diver rotates faster through air with his body tucked in, a skater with her arms held tight to her body. She needed to "visualize" how "change in moment [of inertia] changes the angular velocity." And when that insight came, it was exciting and satisfying. But, for the most part, understanding came too seldom and without a corresponding burst of self-confidence.

Discussion

In fact, as she noted herself, physics was not catering to Vicki's strengths. There was very little opportunity for Vicki to do what she does best: recall long written passages in which important themes are highlighted and elaborated through repetition; discuss in class concepts and ideas; write papers and do independent library or field research; take essay examinations. Just as we in the social sciences could not imagine teaching our courses without some or all of those elements, so the physics instructor could not imagine "mastery" being demonstrated by anything but *increasing skill at problem solving*.

Commenting upon her performance and her field notes, Vicki's professor responded that many of his students, although motivated to succeed in physics, "do not have much curiosity about their mistakes." They don't do the homework problems constructively, standing back to ask themselves "metaquestions" like "what did I learn from this problem?" Or, "what do I need to know to find the solution?" In short, while not retreating from his emphasis on problem solving, the instructor conceded that many students were not getting out of it what was intended. He admitted the pace and the amount of material in introductory physics is formidable. (Students calculate that, averaged over 15 weeks, introductory physics requires 16 hours per week of work including class time, recitation sections, labs, homework, and studying for exams.) Echoing John Rigden, Director of Physics Programs at the American Institute of Physics, and others who say physics instruction should "cover less to uncover more," Vicki's professor opined that if he had the luxury of covering as little as one-third of the material he would have a better result.

We have seen that Vicki was trying to find words and images to help her make sense of the material, and that when something "clicked" she could be as excited as anyone. Although her learning strategies were, for the most part, inappropriate to this method of teaching physics, she was resourceful, a survivor. Although she avoided her instructors, she did seek help in the resource room among her own friends and among fellow students. And she was impressively self-critical of her own failure to understand. But she also has something to tell science faculty about what makes their subjects "hard" and "off-putting" for students like herself, and about what might have made her a more successful and enthusiastic student of physics.

We asked her as part of a final essay to comment more specifically on the "differences" between studying physics and the social sciences and to summarize her own "deficits" as a student of physics. Two points she elaborated on were "study saturation" and "circuit overload."

> More than in social sciences class, I felt the pressure of not falling behind. Once I started to slack off, I would always slow too far down. In social science courses there are stretches of time during which a student may not have to actively study the subject...we can catch up before the exam. If a physics student were to try this, he or she would quickly fail. While this pressure creates discipline, it also leads to mental stress.

As for "deficits," Vicki longed for more "fluency" in calculus and trigonometry. She had been told she could "pick up" what she needed along the way, but found she had to spend too much time filling in the missing mathematics before tackling the physics. She never doubted that she had the capacity to do "analytical thinking," but noted (I think correctly) that what she lacked was experience. The main issue, though, was Vicki's study habits, forged on the other side of the campus.

My study habits turned out to be vastly different from those I would have needed in science. I wanted to read the text, review my notes, and be able to go into the exam and remember-from-words how to solve a problem. Applying these techniques to physics was like trying to bake a cake on canvas. I needed to get my hands on and into the material and work the problems. Even though I knew this was the only way to succeed, I kept having to struggle with my tried-and-true study methods, the ones that work for me in the social sciences.

She also felt, perhaps because the course focused on skills, that the "range of expertise" varied more in her physics course than in social science. She never got over the shock of having students leave a review session in the middle, or just when problem solving was about to begin. It was as if she were in a beginning language class with students, some of whom spoke that language at home. "In social science there are people who are more advanced than others as far as knowledge is concerned," she wrote. "But in science the more advanced are more advantaged. They can better capitalize on their knowledge."

The Female Factor

Vicki was no more a "typical female" than she was a "typical social science" student. Her position in our sample was serendipitous—she simply responded to an announcement—and she did not mention gender issues, except in passing. Still, there are some interesting links between her response to classroom physics and that reported by a recent University of Michigan study of 420 seniors (70 percent female), of whom 182 were science majors and 238 students in other fields.[3]

Women make up 50 percent of the general population and 44 percent of the U.S. work force, but comprise only 13 percent of working scientists and engineers. For this reason alone it is important to examine carefully the factors that cause women to choose science or to drop out. In the University of Michigan study, approximately half the respondents were women who had returned a 1983 Women in Science questionnaire which had been sent to incoming freshwomen who had indicated an interest in science or who had high SAT quantitative scores. The recent survey also included a sample of women who had not responded in 1983 but who fit the categories. For comparison, a

---

[3] Jean D. Manis, Nancy G. Thomas, Barbara F. Sloat, and Cinda-Sue Davis, "An Analysis of Factors Affecting Choices of Majors in Science, Mathematics, and Engineering at the University of Michigan," *CEW* (Center for the Education of Women) *Research Report*, No. 23, July 1989.

sample of senior men with equivalent SAT quantitative scores was also included.[4]

A key finding of the study, and one that corresponds to Vicki's observations about classroom physics, is that the college science classroom is perceived by most women, whether they succeed at and persist in science or not, as an "unfriendly" place to be. More than their male classmates, women appear to be "uncomfortable working in the intensely competitive environment" that characterizes many introductory science classes. The authors speculate that this "unease" may contribute to the higher attrition rate among women considering a science major. In their words, "what may act as a spur to individual achievement for men is a significant deterrent for women."

The authors of the study conclude, as did Vicki about herself, that certain students, among them women and most likely our second tiers, would respond better to science if more "cooperative and interactive modes of learning" were part of the pedagogy, and if scientific knowledge were more closely and explicitly linked to important societal issues. These changes might not have made Vicki a more successful physics student; but then again, they might have.

---

[4] Some 91 percent of those answering the questionnaire were Caucasian, 5.5 percent Asian-American and the remainder divided among black, Hispanic, and native American students.

The Lipson Study

The field notes we collected from our second tier stand-ins are incisive and thought provoking. But two obvious questions remain. First, how likely is it that, even with a welcoming and successful first-year science experience, Eric, Vicki, Tom, Laura, Stephanie, Jacki and Michele would have majored in science, i.e. contributed to a reduction of the projected shortfall? Their grades, their professors' comments, and their obvious enjoyment of physical science suggest that Eric, Jacki, and Tom certainly could have become scientific professionals if they had chosen to. Laura is, as we mentioned, finding her own back door into medical education. But there is no way of "playing back" their college years to answer the question unequivocally.

The other question is even more critical: how *typical* of students who start science and then drop out were our second tier stand-ins? Do we have the right to *generalize* and conclude that their reactions are the same as those of the science students we lose during their college years? Recall that, except for Tom Worthen, none of our second tier stand-ins actually started science in college. If they had, we could not have legitimately employed them as beginning students in physics and chemistry. For different reasons, each was put off by his or her perception of what science studies would entail, or by assessments (their own or others') of their abilities in science. Indeed, with the single exception of Tom, it can be said they never gave college science a chance. So, to get some sense of the degree to which we could extrapolate from our auditors' accounts of their courses, we engaged Abigail Lipson, a psychologist and senior member of the Harvard University Bureau of Study Counsel, to find other relevant sources.

As a more general source of information about the factors that lead able students into or out of science, Dr. Lipson identified *The Concentration Choice Study, 1978-1983*, a data set of Harvard-Radcliffe students done by Susan Bailey, Barbara Burrell and Norma Ware, and available through the archive of the Henry A. Murray Research Center of Radcliffe College.[1] Dr. Lipson suggested that she do a so-called secondary analysis of this data set, particularly of the recorded interview protocols of "switchers" (our term), students who came to college wishing to pursue a science major and then switched to other fields.

The original study tracked 300 Harvard-Radcliffe students. One

[1] We are grateful to the administrators of the Murray Center at Radcliffe for permission granted to Dr. Abigail Lipson and to Research Corporation to use the data set and to review the interview protocols. We have taken care to protect the anonymity of all who participated in the study.

group from the class of 1982 had high science aptitude (measured in part by high math SATs), but exhibited varying degrees of commitment to science as indicated by their prearrival declarations. Another group from the class of 1983 were students who did declare an interest in science, but who exhibited varying degrees of aptitude. Both groups were closely followed through their four years at college and assessed in a variety of ways. Demographic and background data were collected; their academic records were tracked through their four years; they responded to questionnaires about their academic experiences. Students from the 1983 group were administered TATs (thematic apperception tests) to assess various personality variables and, at the beginning of each of their four years, 40 students from each group were interviewed. Finally and most importantly for the Harvard-Radcliffe study and for the comparisons we were seeking, their concentration choices were recorded. The study focused particularly (but not exclusively) on male-female differences and science-nonscience predictors. While some of the findings had previously been published, the interview data had not been analyzed in much depth until Dr. Lipson began her work for us.[2]

We asked Dr. Lipson to do a general review of the findings and then to concentrate on the content of interviews with the group we called the "switchers."[3] We did not ask her to focus particularly on first-year experiences in science courses; indeed, those interviewed had much to say about their courses in all their four yearly interviews. But in her initial report, she already noticed the significance of the first-year course. She wrote:

> The results of the concentration choice study suggest that the pipeline "hemorrhage" consists of more women than men even when other variables (such as preparation, aptitude, or first-year grades) are controlled for...And it suggests that students' first-year experiences are what makes the difference in their ultimate decision about science concentration.

Even students who did not switch out of science had a negative perception of the "classroom climate." The authors of a report on the original study noted that science concentrators tended to rate their

[2] Previous studies include a number of documents filed in the Murray Center. The following have also been published: Norma Ware and Nicole Steckler, "Choosing a Science Major: The Experience of Women and Men," *Women's Studies Quarterly*, XI:2, Summer 1983; Norma Ware, Nicole Steckler, and Jane Leserman, "Undergraduate Women: Who Chooses a Science Major?" *Journal of Higher Education*, Vol. 56, No. 1, Jan./Feb. 1985.

[3] Valerie E. Lee uses this term, too, in her paper, "Identifying Potential Scientists and Engineers: An Analysis of the High School-College Transition," prepared as a contractor report for *Elementary and Secondary Education for Science and Engineering, Grade School to Grad School*, Office of Technology Assessment, U.S. Congress, June 1988.

department of concentration as considerably "less supportive" than other departments, and their fellow concentrators as "less friendly" than nonscience concentrators.[4] Further,

> science concentrators were also less likely to report speaking in classes and feeling free to disagree with their teachers in their concentration courses than in their nonscience courses.

Students also reported that their science courses were considerably "harder" and more time-consuming than Harvard courses in other fields. As juniors, students in the sciences were much more likely to rate courses in their department as difficult (78 percent) than were those in other fields (26 percent).[5] Moreover, in their junior-year questionnaire responses, science concentrators reported feeling that their courses had gotten harder as they progressed, while nonscience students reported feeling that their courses had gotten easier.[6]

Even more telling for our study, the *Concentration Choice Study* revealed that for both men and women *enjoying* a science course more than all their other freshman courses was a significant predictor of their decision to major in science.[7] For uncertain students, freshman year experiences were the *deciding* factors. Also critical was how students explained to themselves the difficulty they were having with science.[8]

> In stating the reasons for their difficulty, science concentrators tended to invoke the "external" explanation, tracing the source of the difficulty to some aspect of the course material, while those who eventually left science were more likely to cite their own inadequacies.

In reviewing the interview transcripts of "switchers," Lipson noted five main themes: 1) a rejection of the "culture of competition;" 2) difficulties in decision-making about the science concentration; 3) fear of cheating themselves of a "well-rounded liberal education;" 4) the complex relationship among *performance, interests* and *motivation;* 5) perceived differences between science and nonscience. What follows are selections from her report to this project.

---

[4] Norma Ware, Jane Leserman and Nicole Steckler, "Aspects of Academic Experience Among Prospective Science Concentrators: A Report on the Concentration Choice Study," Special Projects, Radcliffe College, March 1983, p. 13.

[5] Waren, Leserman, Steckler, *op. cit.*, p. 13, on difficulty; p. 14, on time-consuming.

[6] Ware, Leserman, Steckler, *op. cit.*, p. 13.

[7] Norma Ware and Nicole Steckler, "Choosing a Science Major," *Women's Studies Quarterly* XI:2, Summer 1983, p. 13.

[8] Ware, Leserman, Steckler, *Report, op. cit.*

Theme 1 - Rejection of the "Culture of Competition" in Favor of a "Culture of Competence"

Some students don't decide to reject science per se. They reject the culture of competition that they see as an unavoidable aspect of undergraduate science study. These students don't drop science because they fail in the competition. Often they do very well. Rather for them issues of "culture," in the sense used above, are as important as the actual subject matter of their studies. They value such qualities as love for one's subject and intrinsic motivation in one's work, and want these qualities to be part of their academic efforts. They see the culture of college science study, in contrast, as emphasizing extrinsic rewards like getting good grades, and objective goals like getting into graduate or medical school.[9]

The switchers also want close working relationships with their teachers; they value learning through collaboration and discussion. And they find these, too, missing in the culture of competition which they associate with undergraduate science study. They reject the anonymity of large classes and the isolation of solo work. Instead, they seek very deliberately to be part of a "culture of commitment and competence." In high school they experienced science study in this positive way. In college a different atmosphere dominates and this begins to affect them personally. One student commenting specifically about grade competition told the interviewer:

> When I am around people who are constantly asking "how did you do?" it rubs off on me...I start worrying about the course more for the grade than for the material, which I don't like to do.

Their dislike of the competitive culture and their interest in science come to be in direct conflict. They feel they can't study science and simply ignore the pressurized atmosphere. Yet, they also don't want to seek out more compatible working conditions if it means forgoing their interests in science. Describing this dilemma, one freshman says:

---

[9] The issue of "competition" in science is a tricky one. For one thing, we know that many of the students who reject science will find their way into business or law—highly competitive occupations. Also, while some working scientists believe the competitive classroom to be an appropriate warm-up for what they perceive to be an extremely competitive professional life, others remark that their training and work as scientists have involved just the opposite: pleasure in collaboration. One scientist was quite lyrical in stating his opposition to this finding of the *Concentration Choice Study*. "Trying to understand nature is like an unending jigsaw puzzle game, and it is a great joy to see an ever-increasing fraction of the larger picture evolve regardless of who is successful in fitting a few more pieces. Of course one is greatly pleased if one succeeds a bit oneself, but the main pleasure is to be a small player of this game and part of the scientific community. In that sense, science is amazingly noncompetitive." (Personal communication to the author, not attributed for lack of opportunity to get permission.)

I came here wanting to do biology, but when we had the concentration meeting there were just too many students and I didn't particularly like that. So I started thinking about alternatives...But still, the subject matter I wanted to study most was biology.

Unfortunately, there is no happy ending to this story. After first semester sophomore year, this student switched out of science entirely. Another student blamed the classroom tension on premeds.

[In] Chem 20, you can cut the tension with a knife. [People are] very edgy...I don't know whether it's because of [the premeds] or because of what being a premed makes you become.

Related to the "culture of competition" was the inaccessibility of professors. Students thought they could have overcome the impersonality of the classroom culture if they had been able to develop a relationship with their instructors.

The difference between science courses and [courses in] social studies [is that] I got to know so many more professors on a one-to-one basis. And they are really interested in what you are doing, which is nice.

I prefer smaller courses and smaller departments...because you have a better contact with people.

Theme 2: Decision-Making —"Shooting in the Dark"

Students are influenced in their course choices and their concentration decisions by many people: peers, parents, teachers and advisors. But this advice is often remarkably unhelpful, especially when a student has no way of evaluating it or of putting it to use in an internal process of decision-making.

I took the math placement test and I was on the borderline of Math 1a and Math AR, and they said, "Take Math AR," and so I did that. [Interviewer: Who said that?] The gods from above who sent back the computer readout from the placement test.

[My] advisors are trained to allow the student to make the decision...So one is sort of left on one's own.

[Interviewer: Has anyone you have talked to helped you with your decision?] My roommate is majoring in physics and she tells me almost every day how lucky I am not to be in that department, so that really helps!

75

> [A senior reported that she organized a session for freshmen who were trying to choose concentrations.] I had some of my senior friends come and talk...and it was amazing. One [freshman] said, "Oh, I can't apply to biochemistry," and I said, "why not?" And she said, "because my GPA isn't high enough," and I said, "that's ridiculous!" A friend had told her she needed to have a 3.1 to apply to biochemistry, so she wasn't going to apply.

Students are required to declare a concentration at the end of their freshman year at Harvard-Radcliffe, regardless of how certain or uncertain they may be about their decision. Many students in the population of "switchers" comment on how difficult it is to know what to do when you don't know what to do. And for many students, this uncertainty is a new experience. They entered college with a particular skill or interest in science, but never made an explicit and deliberate commitment to science. They "always knew" that science was something they were good at or something they enjoyed.

By the end of freshman year these students are overwhelmed by all the options they have discovered that they never knew existed before. They could study *anything*! Now they must make a *choice* to pursue science. Often they feel that they have little or no basis on which to make that decision. Yet, they must declare a concentration whether or not they are ready. That's why their decision is often simply a shot in the dark.

> [When] I worked in the clinic I was so carried away with the idea of being a scientist and getting to work with all this fancy equipment that I hardly asked any questions about whether it was really good for me.
>
> I decided to major in biochemistry at the end of freshman year and took a job in a bio lab, my third year in that kind of lab. But then I wanted to try something more theoretical. So I switched this year to physics without ever having had very much physics; it was kind of a shot in the dark.

This student graduated with a humanities degree.

Theme 3: Science Versus Liberal Arts

Many students (especially the premeds in the sample) feared that they could not get a well-rounded education if they majored in science. Some were attracted by fields that they had not gotten to know in high school. Others argued cogently that the liberal arts ought to be a necessary foundation for true scientific achievement in that it would give them greater wisdom and training in different ways of thinking. Early specialization, they feared, would lead to narrow-mindedness and intellectual inflexibility.

Students feel that it is not possible to major in science and get a good liberal arts education for two reasons. First, the competition is too intense. If they major in science they will have to do so single-mindedly, or they will be at a disadvantage in comparison with their more "monkish" classmates. Second, the course requirements are highly sequential. Students who arrive at Harvard-Radcliffe without advanced placement courses or substantial high school backgrounds in science and mathematics have to devote many of their limited elective credits to preparing for, and then completing, the science sequences.

> I see a lot of people in my classes here who have "gone to college" while still in high school, taken courses like this one already. They are math majors because they are two or three years ahead of me. How good a math major am I going to be if I am [already] two years behind?

> I was intimidated by some of the people in the physics department. I started out with Physics 5 and they had started with Physics 55 and Physics 143 and so forth. And I felt like I would never catch up.

Many of the talented science students in the sample who were interested in medicine found a reasonable compromise in taking premed courses while majoring in nonscience areas. One unfortunate outcome, however, is that they miss the advanced courses in science that would have exposed them to research. Hence, they prepare themselves only for clinical medicine and not for academic science.

Theme 4: Performance, Interests, Motivations

In discussing why they switched from science to nonscience concentrations, students most often discuss the complex relationship between their performance, their interests, and their motivations. First, even exceptionally good students can be intimidated by how good "everyone" in science is, and how hard "everyone" works. The sciences must be solely the province of geniuses, they think.

> The grapevine has it that people don't major in math or physics here unless they were child prodigies to begin with. This isn't to say that if I had some overriding desire to do math or physics I wouldn't. But it is something to be overcome.

> Even though I had done really well in the math courses I took here...one of my section leaders told me that only people who start out in Math 55 keep taking math.

> It is really quite a shock when people are so competent. I went into Math 1A first semester, not prepared...and I had to drop back because of the kids who are majoring in science.

There is a feeling here that anyone can do humanities, but not everyone has the discipline to do science. Rumor has it that the IQs of science concentrators are 11 points higher than those of humanities concentrators and that only dummies go into something like English.

Second, students note how profoundly their motivations and interests are affected by their performance rather than the other way around. For many Harvard-Radcliffe students this is their first experience with such discouragement.

I am taking math, but I am not doing too well. If I continue to do poorly, I might very well be tempted to just drop it.

[Interviewer: What didn't appeal to you in physics?] Well, I didn't do well in my physics course. I think that is the major thing that didn't "appeal" to me.

My interest in math is starting to decline. Bad grades make it very difficult to follow interests. That's not the way it should be, but that's the way it is.

A third factor related to performance, interests and motivation is that in a competitive undergraduate environment, indeed in a competitive world environment, doing well becomes an end goal in itself. Students say they are "puzzled" and "disappointed" even as they "learn important lessons" at Harvard-Radcliffe about the relationship between grades, performance, motivation, and personal interests and values.

A science course like physics, chemistry, or biology is a lot more cut-and-dried...in the way you go about problem sets. You can take a course and never really understand it, and still do okay. That happened to me in chemistry freshman year. I was totally fogged out about it and still doing decently.

Grading on a curve, for some of these students, makes decision-making more confusing still.

You can do poorly on a test, know you didn't understand all the material, but when they curve the grade and it comes out to be a "B-plus" you can't help feeling a lot happier about it even though you know it doesn't in any way change how much you knew.

Theme 5: Perceived Differences Between Science and Nonscience

Most students feel there are "inherent differences" between the sciences and the nonsciences. The sciences are more certain, less abstract, more fact-oriented, more memorization-oriented, more focused, more neat and orderly, more predictable, and more analytic, than the nonsciences. In contrast, the nonsciences are perceived by students, particularly those who switch out, to be more self-expressive, more personal and personally relevant, more creative, more understanding-oriented, more expansive, and more "synthetic" than the sciences.

> When I write a paper in literature, it is a way of expressing myself as well as getting the ideas out of the books and down on paper. When I do a problem set, it is more of a mental exercise, taking something formulaic, practicing it, and seeing if I can understand and use it.

> I think a science major is a kind of person who likes to know that, if he knows enough, he will do well. The kind of person who likes social science is a lot more interested in ideas and in concepts.

> [In the humanities] you can go off and expand on things, whereas in the hard sciences you have to come up with a number or a specific word. I used to think of myself as a science type, but I tend now to do better on the expanding.

> Success in science requires analytical thinking and, depending on whether you are in the biological or physical sciences, either a great command of facts or astute problem-solving ability. Humanities tends to be more synthetic and require some personal thought.

Students who stay long enough in science to take higher-level courses begin to see science as more creative, less certain. From an upperclassman:

> Math and especially science are a lot more creative than people believe. Chemistry problems require a lot of creativity, *but of a different type.* There are many [details] and you have to dream up a solution. But it is not mechanical; it takes thought.

But students who switch out of science along the way never discover this truth. "Right-answer science" implies the world is a closed system where only right answers abound. At one level this is correct; at another it is a pedagogical turnoff. Instructors in science are going to have to find ways to convey the excitement inherent in the "logic of discovery" within the "logic" of their most efficient presentation.

Lipson also located a sixth theme, of particular importance to women students, namely the anticipated conflicts between family and career. Since these were not issues our second tier stand-ins addressed directly, we shall not quote any of the interview transcripts at length. But some concerns go beyond women and impinge on student perceptions of the life of a scientist more generally.

When you talk to people who have science careers...you wonder exactly how their family lives are, how much the kids suffer because of it.

The University of Michigan study cited earlier (page 69) confirms much of what Lipson found in the interview transcripts from the *Concentration Choice Study*. Students want more information about job availability, career options, and career alternatives in their own field as compared to other fields. They want to know what is required for different specialties, how to get experience so that they can anticipate what will be the payoffs and pressures of different specializations.[10] That study also corroborates Lipson's and our findings as to the significance of science courses in conveying a sense of what science is like, and of students' perception of the "classroom culture" of college science. At Michigan,[11]

> science students were much more likely than other students to say that science courses were more difficult than other courses, and that science majors have difficulty fitting desired electives into their schedule. Forty-five percent of the students agreed with the complaint that students in science classes are too aggressive and competitive. (Among women who dropped out of science, this factor stood out more than any other as having a differential impact.) Nearly 40 percent agreed with the view that science and math courses are not concerned with "values."

It is clear that, although our second tier stand-ins were not typical of students who switch out of science in terms of their personal biographies, their reactions to the *structures* of their courses, the subject matter, and the pedagogy of introductory science were similar to those of students who start science and then drop out. First tier students may well be teacher-proof, curriculum-proof, and classroom culture-proof, in which case they will learn no matter how the course is taught. In contrast, second tier students must not only do well, they must also feel good about their courses. They require, and I would argue, deserve more attention, more information, and more support.[12]

---

[10] Jean D. Manis, Nancy G. Thomas, Barbara F. Sloat, Cinda-Sue Davis, "An Analysis of Factors Affecting Choices of Majors in Science, Mathematics, and Engineering at the University of Michigan," CEW Research Report #23, July 1989, p. 24.

[11] CEW Research Report # 23, *op.cit.*, p. 19 and p. 21.

[12] For a description of how diffident and uncertain even very able first tier students can be, see "Evaluating a Caltech Education," segment by Rob Fätland, *Caltech News*, Vol. 24, No. 2, April 1990, p. 8. After enduring weeks of unclear lectures in chemistry, "I learned...to say 'I don't understand' as often as I could," he writes.

Final Speculations

> "The biggest and most long-lasting reforms of undergraduate education will come when individual faculty or small groups of instructors adopt the view of themselves as reformers within their immediate sphere of influence, the classes they teach every day."

—K. Patricia Cross[1]

The second tier project only included introductory courses in physics and chemistry and not biology because physical science is where the shortfall is expected to occur and where attrition at the college (and graduate) level is highest. Our auditors were students who might have done science in college, but chose not to. As more mature learners, they found the subjects "fascinating," the teaching adequate (even "good," given the goals of the introductory courses), but not designed to *woo* them or people like them into science. In a postscript to the project, Eric's professor made his assumptions quite explicit: he fully expected his introductory physics students to be already committed to the subject and to want to improve their problem-solving skills. For our auditors, that focus produced a certain *tyranny of technique*. They hungered—all of them—for information about *how* the various methods they were learning had come to be, *why* physicists and chemists understand nature the way they do, and *what* were the *connections* between what they were learning and the larger world.

They also suffered mightily from the absence of community. This was exacerbated both by the large class size common in introductory science and by the lack of a contagious enthusiasm for the subject matter, even among those of their fellow students who were doing well. To be sure, our auditors were not privy to their professors' one-on-one interactions with students who sought them out after class or in office hours. So neither they nor we have any reason to believe that those who we are calling "first tier" (students who even poor teaching might not dissuade from science), were alienated or disappointed by these courses. Those who qualified for the honors chemistry course enjoyed it not least because they had to share their professor's time with only 80 others. Our students, however, needed more attention, more depth, and more excitement.

For some years now, the four-year liberal arts colleges have been

---

[1] K. Patricia Cross is Professor of Education at the University of California, Berkeley.

producing a larger *share* of physical science majors than the research universities.[2] One reason is that they do not, as a rule, offer engineering, agriculture, nursing, or other bachelor of science degrees. Thus, their introductory science courses do not need to function as "service factories" for other degree programs. Another reason is that class size, even at the introductory level, is relatively small and professors readily accessible. They are seriously committed to graduating the students they admit, so they provide the tutoring and support their students need. But surely another factor must be the science departments' need to populate their programs. More than the research universities, the smaller colleges are customer-based. Either they prime the demand for science or they have too few students to teach. Historical data from the all-women's colleges, and more recently from certain all-black institutions, confirm these disproportions.[3] Recruitment has to be intentional at colleges like these, and from their institutions' output data, it appears that it is.

We have to wonder why, in the face of the much touted shortfall, the large research universities have not adopted a similar strategy; why they have not structured their first-year courses not only to introduce the subject, but also to recruit, and above all retain, new students to science. And why, instead, do they allow courses to be taught year after year which weed out (or cause students to weed themselves out) instead of cultivating new students to science? I have already offered one of my speculations (page 9)—the prejudice among faculty members that "true" science students will not need to be appealed or pandered to, but will rise like cream to the top irrespective of what happens in their introductory courses. Other pressures are also at work: 1) it is easier to teach the standard course in the standard way; 2) it is necessary to pack in as much material as possible to prepare students for the next course in the sequence; 3) it is "cost-effective" to gather 300-plus students in a single classroom for one presentation or 600-plus for two sessions back-to-back; and 4) since there are no outside teaching funds with which to pay skilled native English speakers to lead the laboratories and recitation sections, it is necessary to employ graduate students who have been selected on criteria very different from teaching, however impoverished their instructional skills...And so on.

---

[2] Jerry P. Gollub and Neal B. Abraham, "Physics in the Colleges", *Physics Today,* June 1986, 28-34. The issue for science more generally was featured at the June 1985 "Future of Science at Liberal Arts Colleges" conference held at Oberlin College, Oberlin, Ohio.

[3] M. Elizabeth Tidball and Vera Kistiakowsky, "Baccalaureate Origins of American Scientists and Scholars, *Science,* 193, 4254, Aug. 1976, 646-652. On the women's colleges and female achievement more generally, see also by M. Elizabeth Tidball, "Women's Colleges and Women Achievers Revisited," *SIGNS,* 5, 3, Spring 1980, 504-517. On the role of the historically black colleges and universities, see Julia Clark, "The Status of Science and Mathematics in Historically Black Colleges and Universities," *Science Education,* 69 (5): 673-679; 1985.

But as this project progressed, I began to wonder whether these physical science professors know something we don't know, namely that the projected shortfall may be just that: projected, not certain; and that, like the American Medical Association, the profession feels it is better served by keeping standards high and members few. Mindful of the devastating effects of the oversupply of physicists in the 1970s, a situation which drove many good Ph.D.s permanently out of the field, many physicists tell me mournfully, "there has never been a time when there were too few physicists." What they may be thinking is this: until and unless there is a palpable increase in *demand* for working scientists, the shortfall remains a prediction and not yet a reality.

How certain are we that the nation will experience such a shortage of trained scientists in the first decades of the next century? On what basis has the shortfall been calculated? And have not those who frame the agenda possibly confounded two issues, the nation's *need for more science* with a *need for more scientists?* The first is a political and economic imperative. The second could be little more than wishful thinking. Or, to say it differently, if we think the nation needs more science (which most thinking people believe to be the case), should we not be focusing on increasing the *demand* for science workers, instead of focusing exclusively on increasing the *supply?*[4]

Most of the shortfall is extrapolated from demographic projections and the composition of the so-called talent pool. The calculations are obtained by multiplying the population of college-age people in the birth cohort by the historical proportion of college students, by sex and minority composition, who major in science and engineering.[5] Since the cohort of 18-year-olds has been declining since 1980 when it stood at 4.5 million, and will continue to do so until 1995 when it will total 3.25 million, there is concern about the size of the natural pipeline. (It will only rise again, to 4 million, in the year 2005.) Also of concern is that between 1990 and 2000, in the smaller cohorts, the proportion of black and Hispanic youngsters will increase to one-quarter of their age group; and that these are the ethnic groups which have not historically produced many scientists or engineers. The resulting prediction is of a "declining output of scientists and engineers...inevitable personnel shortages in certain fields of science and engineering."[6]

---

[4]Betty Vetter, science human resources specialist, in a private communication to the author, puts this very succinctly: "Demand," she writes, "equals need with funding added. It doesn't make any difference how many scientists and engineers we need to solve our myriad problems, demand is not created until money is available to pay for their services. Thus, any forecast of demand or of supply-demand imbalance, must rest on some assumptions about the level of expenditure (by local, state and federal government, by industry, or by academe) to attain some objective."

[5] *Educating Scientists and Engineers: From Grade School to Grad School*, U.S. Congress, Office of Technology Assessment, 1989. See p. 8 for an explanation of how this is done.

[6] From the National Science Foundation's *The Science and Engineering Pipeline*, PRA Report 87-2, April 1987, pp. 1-2.

Although the authors of most of the shortfall projections caution against drawing "safe conclusions about future supplies of scientists and engineers [solely] on the basis of aggregate demographic trends...,"[7] supply projections tend to dominate the discussion. As for future "demand," the authors concede that *market forces* will be critical, and that the best that government can do is to "ensure a baseline *capacity* to adjust to market changes." In fact, there is more controversy surrounding the shortfall projections than has so far made its way into the popular press. In an interview with Betty Vetter, director of the Commission on Professionals in Science and Technology (a demographics affiliate of the AAAS), A. K. Finkbeiner quotes her as saying that information on the present supply and present demand is "not very good, and projections into the future stink."[8] "Just because the college-age cohort is going to get smaller," OTA's Nancy Naismith says in the same article, "doesn't necessarily mean there's a problem. Demographics isn't destiny." Alan Fechter of the National Research Council is even more critical. He calls the projections "worst case scenarios" because they do not allow for market responses and adjustments. Industrial demand, with 54 percent of all scientists in its employ, is the least predictable; colleges and universities whose retirements are known, the most. But higher education employs only 25 percent of all scientists (14 percent work in government and other agencies; the rest are scattered). Fechter thinks *no one* knows what the demand from industry will look like in the 1990s. "...Higher probably, but how much higher we don't know."[9]

Let's return now to our science professoriat. What factors might they see influencing *demand* in the coming decades?

While the "R," for research in military "R and D," has always comprised a much lower portion than the "D" for development, overall reductions in defense outlays will surely reduce the *demand* for physical scientists and the amount of research money available to them. Apart from direct cuts to the national weapons laboratories, to research universities, and to other research institutions, any decline in production orders will also reduce the size of the defense work force. This sector of the economy contains a higher proportion of scientific and technical talent than the national labor force as a whole. So unless

---

[7] OTA Report, *op., cit*, p. 9

[8] All quotes in this paragraph except for the "worst case scenario" comes from A. K. Finkbeiner, "Demographics or Market Forces?" *Mosaic*, Vol. 18, No. 1, Spring 1987, p. 10. Fechter's "worst case scenario" remark was made during his presentation at the AAAS National Meeting, New Orleans, Feb. 17, 1990.

[9] Still, Richard C. Atkinson, President of AAAS, predicts a shortfall of 450,000 science and engineering B.A.s by 1995 and 700,000 by 2010. While he concedes that there is a considerable range in the projection of the annual shortfall of Ph.D.s (950-9,600), he takes the higher figure to be the most realistic. These data are taken from Richard C. Atkinson, "Supply and Demand for Scientists and Engineers..." presidential address, AAAS National Meeting, New Orleans, Feb. 18, 1990, tables on pp. 10a and 17a respectively.

the "peace dividend" finds it way directly or indirectly into support for civilian technologies, this labor force will be diminished, too.[10]

It is beyond the scope of this essay to describe how the United States might *prime the demand* for science by way of public and private sector financing. Comparisons with West Germany and Japan are, however, instructive. West German industry, its federal government and Laender (states) together invested $33.2 billion in science research in 1989, of which 35 percent came from the public and nonprofit sectors and 65 percent from industry. Japan's commitment to civilian R and D is well documented. Both countries invest just under 3 percent of total GNP in research and development, by far the bulk of it civilian (85 percent for West Germany, 97 percent for Japan). The payoff is immediate (in terms of numbers of new patents granted) and long-term. Japan's rate of research investment need not be chronicled here. But *The Economist* last fall characterized West Germany's recent performance as meriting that country *Wissenschaftswunder* status, a play on the German *Wirtschaftswunder* of two decades ago.[11]

To return to my argument, those who are focusing on the science crisis in the schools assume a steady, even an increasing demand, and a diminishing supply. The science professoriat may be reading the signals differently and anticipating, instead, an uncertain or temporary demand, whatever the supply.

And what of the students themselves? What is their perception of future *demand*? As Kenneth Green remarks in his review of the freshman and follow-up surveys of undergraduate interest and career plans:[12]

> Paralleling the declining interest in the sciences has been a
> bull market in business. Between 1972 and 1988 the propor-
> tion of freshmen planning to pursue business careers more
> than doubled...Currently one-fourth of the college freshmen
> surveyed plan to major in business...business now accounts
> for about one-fourth of all undergraduate degrees awarded.

While some may dismiss this as "greedy materialism," students are reading the signals, too. Business promises not just money, but em-

---

[10] Cuts in the armed forces will inevitably cause reductions in the demand for military officers. And this could be followed by reductions in ROTC, the nation's largest dedicated scholarship program and on many campuses the only one that favors undergraduate majors in science, mathematics, and engineering. ROTC scholarships increased from 80,000 to 110,000 between 1979 and 1989, a figure that could be reversed in the coming decade. See Leslie F. Malpass, "The Benefits of ROTC on Campus: A President's Perspective," *The Educational Record*, Winter, 1985, 15-18. For a prediction of how ROTC might be cut, see also Phil Keisling and Jonathan Alter, "35 Ways to Cut the Defense Budget," *Washington Monthly*, vol. 21, (3) Feb. 1989, p. 50.

[11] "Ein Wissenschaftswunder?", *The Economist,* Nov. 11, 1989, pp. 103-106.

[12] Center for Education Statistics, 1987, p. 105, quoted in Kenneth C. Green, "A Profile of Undergraduates in the Sciences," *The American Scientist,* Sep.-Oct. 1989, 475-480.

ployability, mobility, advancement, and satisfying work. So long as there is no consensus as to what the future holds for science majors, can we responsibly *promise* them a good work life? The assumption here is that the shortfall will happen, and that there will be a ready market for scientists and engineers in the years ahead. But whether the prognosticators are right or wrong, we need to do more to woo students to science if only as a minor subject in the vital interest of improved science literacy.

Recommendations

"Science education policy is not made by government; it is made by college science departments."

—Shirley Malcom[13]

There is no agreement as to the number of students "prepared" to study science in college. From a variety of sources it seems reasonable to conclude that 14 percent of all high school students graduate with courses in physics and chemistry, as well as required biology, under their belts. And this 14 percent provides one measure of the pool of students who could *potentially* be recruited and retained in science at college. But there are different ways of measuring "potential." Hans Andersen, president of the National Science Teachers' Association, was quoted recently as saying that only seven percent of the nation's high school graduates are "ready to pursue science programs" at college (in contrast to the Soviet Union where, he alleges, 85 percent are "prepared").[14] But whether our potential is half a million students per year or half of that, it is considerably more than the number we are currently graduating with college majors in science. So our work is cut out for us. Where do we begin?

The first step is a moral and strategic imperative: no college student should be permitted to say "no" to science without a struggle. This will involve some forays into the comfortable prejudice-laden views of the science professoriat, many of whom (but not all)[15] believe that one has

---

[13] Shirley Malcom is head of the Directorate for Education and Human Resources Programs of the American Association for the Advancement of Science. She made this comment during a discussion of human resources in science at the AAAS National Meeting, New Orleans, Feb. 16, 1990.

[14] Stated in a public lecture in Seattle, Washington, by Hans Andersen, professor of science and environmental education at Indiana University, according to an AP story datelined April 7, 1989.

[15] Nobel laureate Leon Lederman, director emeritus of Fermilab, likes to say of his own career that "being average" was not a disadvantage, and that it was not until five years after his Ph.D. that he began to feel competent. Most scientists are not "brilliant," he says of his colleagues. In fact many "brilliant" people are superficial. The decisive factor is "their ability and willingness to do hard work." Leon M. Lederman, "Low Pay and Long Hours," Reference Frame Column, *Physics Today*, Jan., 1990, p. 9-11.

to have a "mathematical mind" or a "scientific bent" to do science. No longer can we afford binary classifications of students into those who can do science and those who can't and *never will*.

Recruitment and especially ongoing support for any student who crosses the classroom threshold into science should be a conscious and conscientiously pursued goal of introductory courses in science. If scientists don't know how to do this, they should take advice from people who do. As part of this pursuit, the issue of class size has to be addressed anew. There is much conflicting literature on the effects of class size, but one finding is indisputable: that class size and teaching methods are inextricably linked.[16] Science professors in particular may resist small classes because they associate "teaching" with lecturing in a hall filled with students. From *The Chronicle of Higher Education* comes a tale of a young female assistant professor of biology at a large state university who[17]

> ...conducted her biology class by having the students work in small groups. The class was prepared for the lesson and was comfortable with that strategy. A senior faculty member who was observing the junior faculty member stood up shortly after the students assembled themselves in groups and said, loudly enough for all to hear, "I'll come back when you're teaching."

The evaluation this young woman later received, according to the narrator of her tale, was "negative and discouraging." The senior professor complained that there was "too much interaction in class" and that she "didn't use the blackboard enough." One wonders what the students, first tier and second alike, thought of her teaching style.

All students who decide to leave science should be given "exit interviews" conducted by someone within the department. Such interviews can provide the faculty with opportunities to persuade them and to win some number back, or at least give them a chance to suggest other science-related enterprises, such as science teaching or science journalism. More important, student feedback collected from such interviews can be incorporated into the next round of improvements in the science offerings, in the "classroom climate," and in the quality of teaching within the department.

If the science professoriat cannot find the time or the expertise to undertake these added duties, a new cadre of professionals, trained in both science and counseling, should be recruited to act as "science advisors." Just as junior and senior high school counselors, most of whom do not study science in college, cannot adequately "sell" science to our young people, so neither can collegewide deans and career

---

[16] W. J. McKeachie, "Class Size, Large Classes, and Multiple Sections," *Academe* (66), Feb. 1980, 24-27.

[17] From an op. ed. in *The Chronicle of Higher Education*, by Elizabeth Berry, June 21, 1989.

counselors who don't know (firsthand) either the joys of science study or the career opportunities that await. If necessary then, we must provide funds to support department-specific personnel who know science, like science, and who are willing to locate and to monitor job opportunities for science majors. They should consider the needs of terminal B.A.s, those headed for the M.A., and those inclined to seek other advanced degrees. Such professionals could assist faculty in mounting "welcome workshops" and introductory science "support seminars."[18] In addition, they could conduct or simply arrange group tutorials for students having difficulty, advise and counsel those who are wavering in their commitment to science, conduct the "exit interviews" mentioned above, and generally provide the missing human contact and community for students who are not "younger versions" of the science professoriat. With proper status and support, a professional cadre of science advisors could also participate on teaching-assignment committees and act as a force for curriculum reform in their departments.

Resident advisors and other undergraduate support staff should be specifically recruited from among science majors to be the role models, to teach "survival strategies," and to advise beginning students interested in science. Or, if the advisors are not science majors, provision should be made for special training so that they can be of use to underclassmen and women interested in science. From these support staff members could come a body of recommendations to students, recommendations that our second tier stand-ins had to discover on their own: namely, that it is necessary to study hard and continuously in science; that it helps enormously to have a group of friends to work with all the time; that there can be no falling off of effort to be "made up" later on; that it is "legal," even advisable to consult another textbook for clarification; and that students can help themselves and their instructors by writing out their questions about the material and asking for written response if the instructor does not allow sufficient time for questioning in class.

But most importantly, the science faculty must find a way to provide the welcome and success nontraditional science students require *in the classroom*. Freshman science should become again what it once was: the most exciting, mind-expanding course in the curriculum. "Switchers," according to Lipson's reading of the Harvard-Radcliffe protocols, and our second tier stand-ins need to *enjoy* their science courses. This does

---

[18] One model is being tried at Rollins College in Winter Park, Fla. where 25 freshmen taking two or more courses in science and/or college calculus are guided through their first year in science. They attend a seminar where fundamental issues in science and problems in learning science are given equal emphasis. Another is the California MESA program directed toward increasing the number of minority graduates in engineering and computer science. The program is discipline based and emphasizes "community," academic workshops, group student and peer support. See "Keeping Minds in Motion: The Schooling of Minority Engineers," *The College Board Review*, No. 153, Fall, 1989, pp. 41-45, 55.

not mean those courses should be made easy or watered-down. Eric, Jacki, Vicki, Michele, Stephanie, Tom, and Laura wanted more rather than less challenge, but of a different kind. For them, their courses— particularly their exams—were diminished in scope and value by what they called the *tyranny of technique*. Baldly stated, they were of insufficient *intellectual* content to appeal to their wide-ranging minds and interests. As K. Patricia Cross and Dudley Herschbach put it, coming from different disciplinary vantage points, the "grand reform" in college science education, if it is to take place at all, must happen there, in the classroom, where the professor comes to teach and the students come to learn.

Given the intellectual hierarchies of the disciplines of chemistry and physics and the reluctance of most departments to extend the time spent on introductory material, it will not be easy to slow the pace or expand the coverage in these standard courses so as to include history, context, and the larger "vision" of the subjects that would have satisfied our second tier stand-ins. It could be said that entire majors in chemistry and physics embrace a standard curriculum, not just the introductory courses. Moreover, since the subject matter to a large extent dictates the teaching style (particularly in large classes), any perturbation of pedagogy, it will be argued, will perforce have a (negative) impact on coverage. Still, there are faculty everywhere trying to reform their courses, even to meet the needs of a wider range of students. Why, then, have innovations in college science teaching so little staying power? One reason, physicist Arnold Arons believes, derives from the prevalence of introductory texts that slight the crucial questions of "how do we know...?" and "why do we believe...?"[19] But another, one that our outside observers were particularly sensitive to, has to do with the limits and deficiencies of in-class testing.[20]

With the exception of Vicki, the students in our experiment did very well on their tests in introductory physics and chemistry, but to a person, didn't like them. Eric found his exams requiring only "a simple exhibition of skills acquired." For Tom, there were "no new conceptual challenges" to get him to think new thoughts on the exams, and for Vicki, as she herself noted, the exams did not play to her strengths. Michele contrasted her physics exams with those she was concurrently setting for her introductory philosophy students. In philosophy, she commented, professors expect their students to do more than they have previously shown themselves capable of doing, not less. Indeed, exams in any college subject are more than a necessary prod to keep students working and up to date. They are the expression in earnest of

---

[19] Arnold Arons, "Uses of the Past: Reflections on U.S. Physics Curriculum Development, 1955-1985" unpublished paper available from the author, Department of Physics, FM-15, University of Washington, Seattle, Wash. 98195.

[20] Arons, *op. cit.*, p. 10.

what the instructor really values, how he or she really measures "mastery."

Sometimes professors are unaware of how much they are communicating by the content and style of the examinations they set. They will lay out an impressive array of goals and objectives for their courses, making certain that their students know that "understanding" goes beyond "right answers." Some will assign extra reading in the history of their subject or encourage students to look over case studies of real-world applications. Others will add films and state-of-the-art video presentations during class time.[21] Yet, students will not be motivated to take all this "extra work" seriously (including their professors' interesting spoken asides) if none of it ever appears as part of homework assignments or on exams. In other words, unless instructors implement their "goals" by including nontraditional questions on homework assignments and exams, students know full well they do not really matter.

In his review of twenty years of curriculum reform in physics, Arons concludes that "...Deficiency in the quality of test questions has been one of the most serious ills of our profession."[22]

> Although there is an extensive (and occasionally perceptive) literature about testing, its influence has not been great. The true intellectual goals of a course are set not in the prospectus, or by the text, but by the tests that are administered. As long as the tests are specious, the intellectual goals remain remote. At the Trieste meeting in 1980, Peter Kennedy characterized this problem in a particularly forceful and disturbing way: he remarked that he sensed a damaging collusion between students on the one hand and faculty on the other—a collusion in which students agreed to accept bad teaching provided they were given bad examinations.

When I was working in the area of mathematics anxiety and avoidance (1975-1987), I would frequently and not entirely in jest suggest to the mathematics education community that to retain "different" kinds of students in mathematics, math tests be graded in the following way: one-third credit for the right answer, one-third (elastic) credit for finding more than one way to get to that answer, and one-third credit for a paragraph-long essay about what makes the particular problem mathematically interesting. Although mathematicians admit that "going from an answer to a question" is the real stuff of mathematical thinking,[23] rarely did I find a mathematics instructor favorably inclined to adopt my grading system. It didn't take them very long to realize that a student could get the right answer, do it in the "right way" and

---

[21] Such as "The Mechanical Universe" produced by David Goodstein.

[22] Arons, *op. cit.*, p. 19.

[23] Personal communication from algebraist Peter Hilton to the author.

get no more than 40 percent credit, i.e., flunk! But students outside mathematics, students who dislike or are fearful of mathematics, invariably found the idea attractive. Many believed that they would be able to write a good essay even if they got the answer wrong. This means they have considerable confidence in their ability to locate what is "interesting" about a problem, and this very often keeps them from proceeding swiftly to an answer; they are simply too easily distracted by these "ancillary" thoughts.

It is hardly appropriate for someone outside of science to propose the specifics either of new kinds of test questions or of new systems of grading, particularly when it is often departments outside of physics and chemistry or standardized tests (like the MCATS) that determine both the content and the mode of evaluation. But it is, I think, appropriate to point out how disappointing (even boring and alienating) it is for students of a certain temperament and mind set to deal with homework assignments and examinations that do not cause them to think "new thoughts."

Of our second tiers' mathematical competence and its relation to their success or lack of success in doing introductory physics and chemistry, one last observation needs to be made explicit. The ones who had the least trouble with introductory science were those whose mathematics skills were either recently exercised or, for other reasons, strong. While inadequacy in mathematics is not by itself a cause of failure to succeed in science, it surely appears to contribute to the degree of difficulty our otherwise very able students experienced. From this, one policy recommendation might be that emphasis be placed on early and continuous exposure to higher and higher levels of mathematics for the *majority* of students in middle school and high school. Such exposure would be on the premise that mathematics competence may be even more important and more useful to success in college science than exposure to more precollege years of science itself. The earlier students have had calculus, says Lynne Abel, associate dean of the College of Arts and Sciences of her students at Cornell University, the greater their success in college science.[24] This means that able students, and not just the ones who show an early interest or ability in science, should be discouraged from (perhaps even prohibited from) dropping out of mathematics at every choice point along the educational continuum.

If we are to open the gates to the second tier, we must not fail to open them early. This does not mean that the pressure for reform of college science is any less. But it does mean that when we populate early identification and enrichment programs we extend our notions of "who does science and why" to include students who have not (yet) displayed an interest or talent for science, i.e. who do not (yet) look like

---

[24] Personal communication to the author.

91

"science types." Too often special programs for early achievers, male or female, majority or minority, are restricted to somebody's notion of what a science student looks like at age 8 or 11 or 16. Rather, these programs should be deliberately expanded to include students who are highly verbal, of broad interests and talent, and otherwise performing well in school. Indeed, one way to satisfy skeptics who doubt that there exists a second tier of intelligent pupils who can be wooed into science would be to have program directors maintain separate records of the achievements of their "less likelies." My hunch is that even students not yet *demonstrably* inclined to science will respond positively to special attention, curriculum enrichment, and personal opportunity. Moreover, this extended recruitment will convey an important message to parents, teachers and students alike, namely that science is a field in which people of diverse interests and backgrounds can find satisfaction and success.

Not all students "prepared" to do science can be recruited to science no matter how much we do for them. It would be foolish to claim that they could. There will always be students who, as Eric said of himself, "discover other loves" in college, and students who, though they like and do well at science, see it not as an end in itself, but rather as a means to some other useful end—medicine, nursing, pharmacology, environmental policy, patent law, engineering, and, above all, science literacy. But there still remain, I believe, a number of students who could be recruited and retained if they were made to feel, as Stephanie put it so well, that there is something science could give to them and something they could give back to science.

And, until we know who they are, we dare not decide in advance who they are not.

About the Author

Sheila Tobias has made a science and an art of being a curriculum outsider. Neither a mathematician nor a scientist, she has tackled the question of why intelligent and motivated college students have task-specific disabilities in certain disciplines, particularly mathematics and science. From her work have come three books (the last in the writing): *Overcoming Math Anxiety* (1978), *Succeed with Math* (1987), and (with physicist Carl T. Tomizuka) *Breaking the Science Barrier*. She is the creator of the technique, "Peer Perspectives on Teaching," in which faculty from fields other than science and mathematics "stand in" for students in artificially constructed science and mathematics lessons at the college level. From their responses to the instruction have come important insights into what makes science and mathematics "hard" and even "distasteful" for outsiders.

Educated in history and literature at Harvard-Radcliffe and Columbia Universities, Ms. Tobias has been a lecturer in history and political science at the Universities of Arizona and of California, San Diego, a college administrator at Cornell and Wesleyan Universities, and a trustee of Stephens College, a woman's college in Columbia, Mo. Her work in science and mathematics avoidance and anxiety has been funded by the Lilly Endowment, the Rockefeller and Ford Foundations, and the Fund for the Improvement of Postsecondary Education in the Department of Education, as well as by Research Corporation.

Selected Bibliography

Overcoming Math Anxiety (W.W. Norton, 1978, Houghton Mifflin in paperback, 1980). *Succeed with Math: Every Student's Guide to Conquering Math Anxiety* (The College Board, 1987). *Breaking the Science Barrier*, with Carl T. Tomizuka (in preparation; The College Board, 1992).

Articles: "Why is a smart girl like you counting on your fingers," *MS.* magazine, September, 1976. "Who's afraid of math and why?" *The Atlantic*, September, 1978. "Anxiety and mathematics: an update", (with Carol Weissbrod), *Harvard Educational Review*, Vol. 50, No. 1, Spring, 1980, 63-39. "Sexist equations," *Psychology Today*, January, 1982. "Math anxiety and physics: the problem of teaching 'difficult' subjects." *Physics Today*, Vol. 38, No. 6, June, 1985, 61-68. "Peer perspectives on teaching," *Change Magazine*, Spring, 1986. "Peer perspectives on physics," *The Physics Teacher*, Vol. 26, No. 2, Feb. 1988, 77-80. "Professors as physics students: what can they teach us?" with R.R. Hake, *American Journal of Physics*, 56 (9), Sept., 1988, 786-794. "Poetry for physicists," *American Journal of Physics*, accepted for publication fall 1990.

Research Corporation: Background
A FOUNDATION FOR THE ADVANCEMENT OF SCIENCE

One of the first U.S. foundations and the only one wholly devoted to the advancement of science, Research Corporation was established in 1912 by scientist, inventor and philanthropist Frederick Gardner Cottrell with the assistance of Charles Doolittle Walcott, secretary of the Smithsonian Institution. Its objectives: to make inventions "more available and effective in the useful arts and manufactures," and "to provide means for the advancement and extension of technical and scientific investigation, research and experimentation..."

Cottrell's inspiration—he was a physical chemist at the University of California—was to create Research Corporation to develop his precipitator and other inventions, particularly those from universities, and to devote any monies realized to grants for scholarly research.

Research Corporation grants are made to support scientific inquiry in physics, chemistry and astronomy at public and private undergraduate institutions (the Cottrell College Science Grants); to assist midcareer chemists, astronomers and physicists in Ph.D.-granting university science departments (Research Opportunity Awards); and to aid projects with promise for advancing science that do not fall under other program guidelines (General Foundation Grants). A new program, Partners In Science, aims to improve high school science education by giving secondary teachers opportunities to do summer research at local colleges and universities.

Grants applications from college and university scientists are reviewed by referees suggested by applicants and supplemented, as appropriate, by the foundation. A final reading of applications and recommendations for approval or denial is given by an advisory committee of academic scientists.

Both the Partners In Science program and the research which led to *They're Not Dumb, They're Different—Stalking the Second Tier* are responsive to a new foundation goal, formulated in 1987, "to increase the flow of young people into the sciences with programs that are appropriate to the foundation's interest and expertise."

Research Corporation grants are supported by an endowment created many years ago by the sale of the electrostatic precipitation business, and by donations from other foundations, industrial companies and individuals wishing to advance academic science. The day-to-day conduct of programs "to make inventions more available and effective" is carried out by Research Corporation Technologies, the foundation's nonprofit sister organization.

Research Corporation's main office is located at 6840 East Broadway Boulevard, Tucson, Arizona 85710-2815.